First published in the UK

ArtistAnd

Hey you creative buggar. I'm wondering if this is the first time you've picked up an art book, or maybe you've dabbled and you wanna explore. Whatever the case, I've written some words and drawn some pictures to help you enjoy shading and become more confident. If you find any spelling mistakes it's just proof that this was made by an artist so embrace the mistakes and let's get cracking!

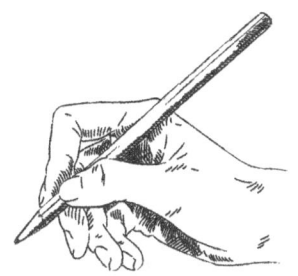

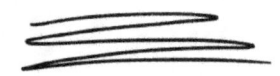

Whose It For?

Perfect for beginners and people who like shading or want to get better without having to think too hard. I'll take you through a series of exercises and drawings that have been tried and tested to hundred of students that I think you'll love and hopefully become addicted too. The best thing about this book, is you can be an absolute novice and still join in!

What's Inside?

Each page of this book contains a different image for you to shade. Some of the images are easy, while others are a tad more challenging. Take your time and shade each image in by following the guide on the reference pages. The book is split up into three sections: **hard edges** and **soft** edges and blending the squares in.

Benefits of Shading

Shading can have many benefits for both your mind and body. For example, did you know that shading can help reduce stress levels? Studies have shown that taking even just 15 minutes out of your day to focus on something calming such as shading, can help lower your stress levels. This could be the new one of your 5 a day?

What You'll Need

Pencils

I recommend you use a 2B & 8B pencil because they're the only two pencils you'll ever need... (in this book anyway). You can get these from your local art shop, in a pack, or from the website. www.artistand.co.uk.

Paper

I suggest you shade inside the book and treat it like one of those mindful colouring books. If you want to re-draw the images you can always get a sketchbook and do it free hand. You'll be a ruddy expert in no time.

Smudging

Some people may want to protect the pencil from smudging so here's a tip for you:

1. Place a piece of paper over the drawing whilst you're shading (just under your hand). This stops your sweaty palm from smudging the pencil.

2. When the drawing is finished, you can add a bit of tissue paper in between the pages so the pencil doesn't rub off on the other page.

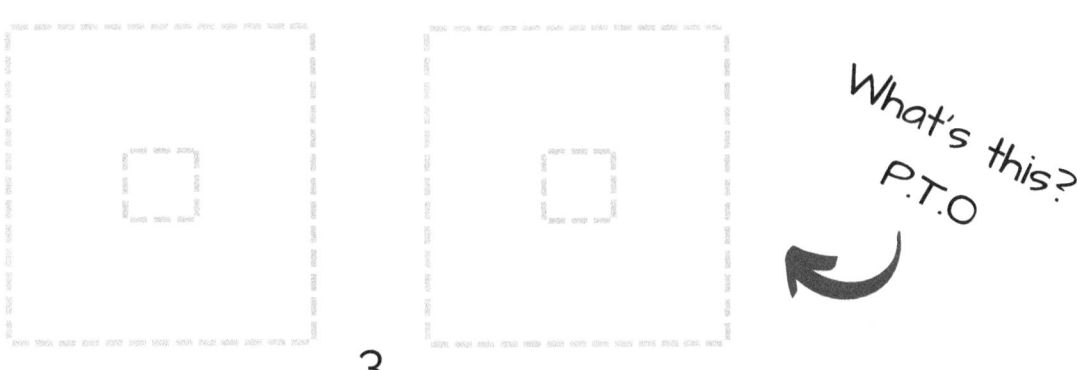

What's this? P.T.O

View Finders

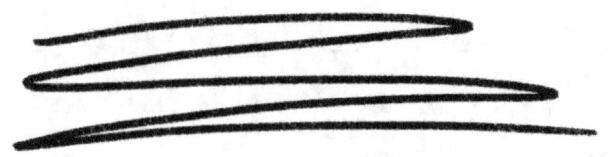

If you want to check your progress and whether you're reaching your shades, make these lil view finders or chop them outta the book.

You can mix and match your viewfinders to have one on your artwork and the other on your original picture or value scale (That'll be explained in a page or so's time).

The aim of these are to help you isolate a shade so you can see how light or dark it is compared to the original picture! Super handy to make sure your eyes don't cheat.

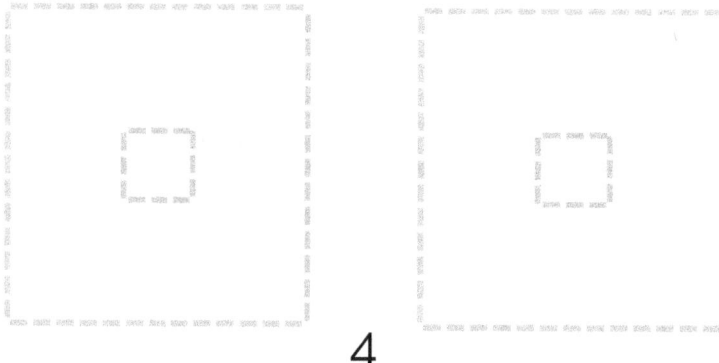

How To Use Them

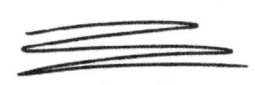

1.

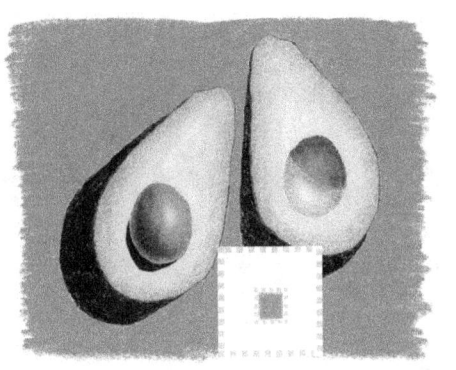

Place one view finder on the reference picture.

2.

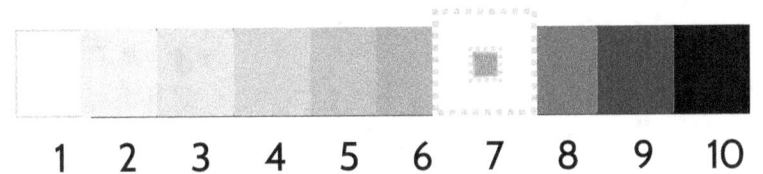

Place the second view finder on the scale to match the shade.

3.

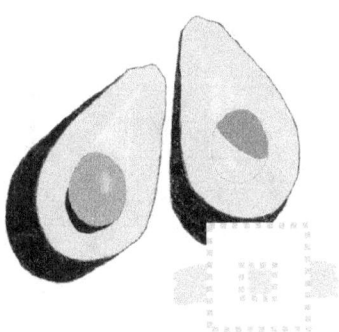

Now move one of the view finders to your drawing to see if it's the same.

5

Try It

Match the squares to the value scale.

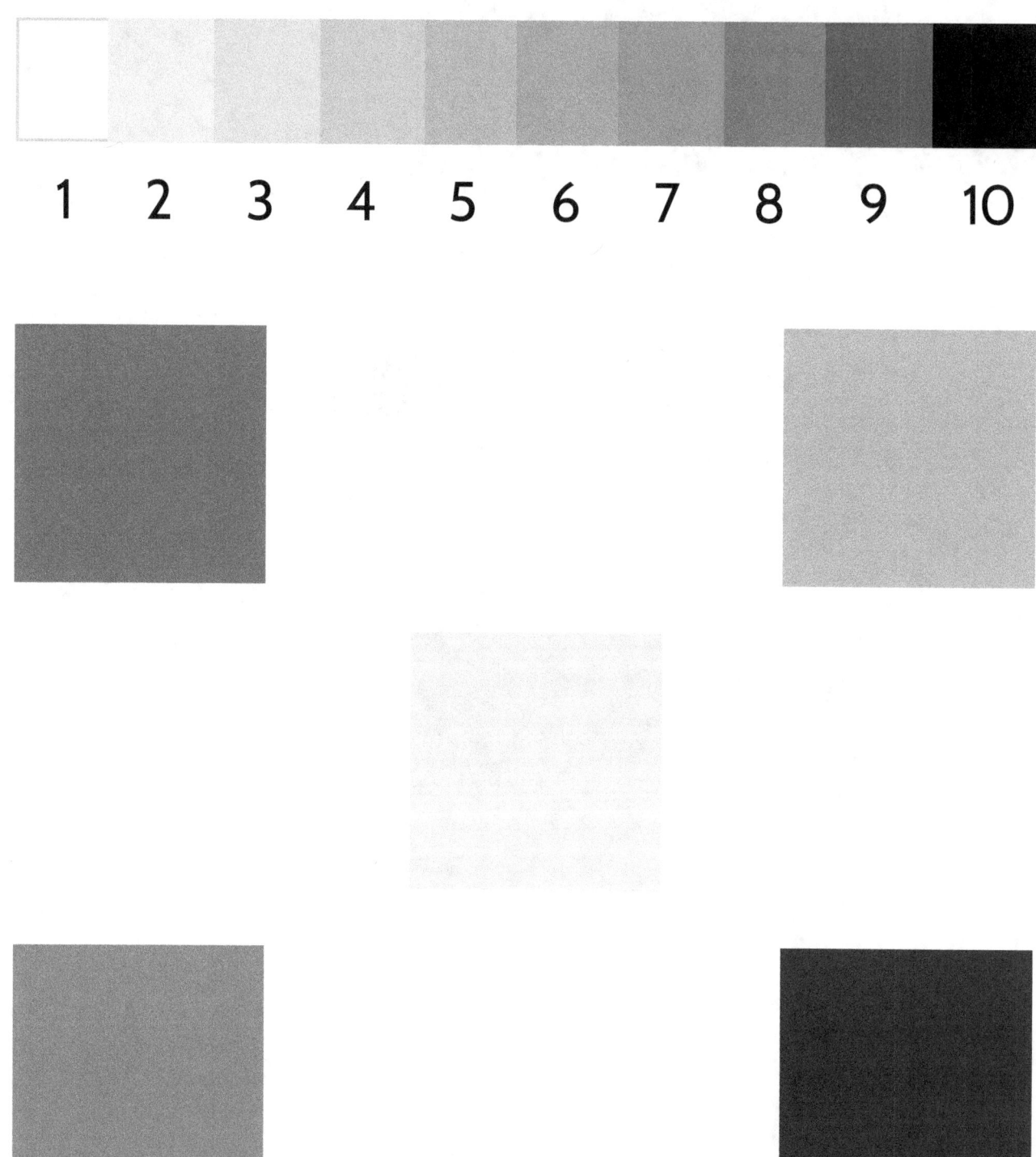

1   2   3   4   5   6   7   8   9   10

Two artists had an art contest.
It ended in a draw.

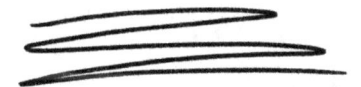

How To Hold Your Pencil

Dark Fine Lines

Hold the pencil close to the tip as if you're writing your name with a pen. This will give you strong sharp lines and darker tones.

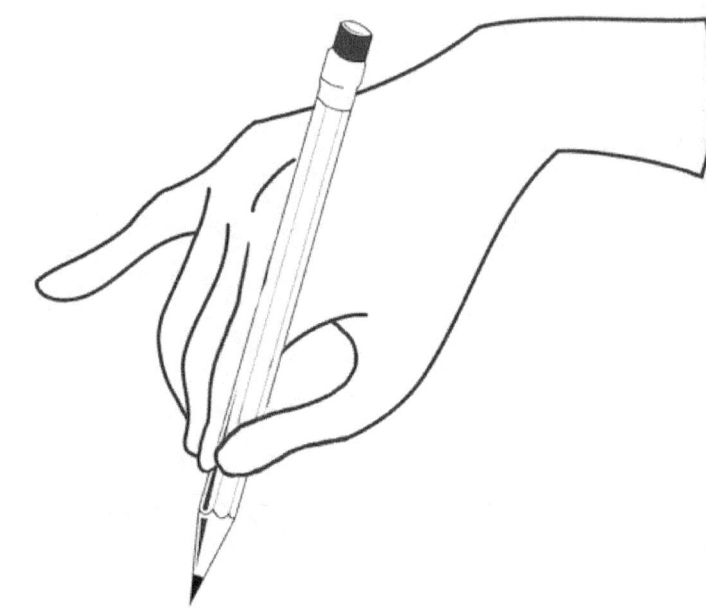

Lighter Softer Lines

Hold the pencil further from the tip in a looser grip. The further you are from the end, the more you use the edge of the lead to make softer gradients

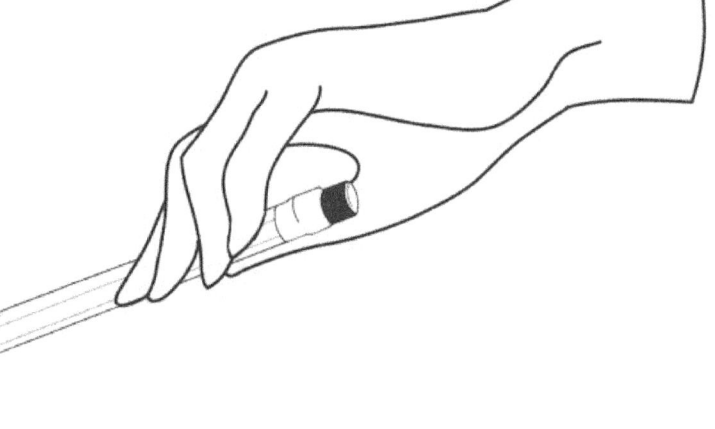

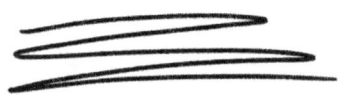

Shading is important for making things look 3D so we want to help you become more confident without having to think too hard! You're going to get better at shading without even realising it! Enjoy these exercises and see how you get better and better in. no time!

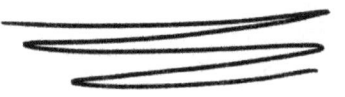

Who's the king of the pencil case? The ruler.

Block Shading

2B Vs 8B Pencil

Strong contrast is the best thing for making something look realistic. So let's practise. This is what the big wigs call a 'value scale', a scale of light and dark. We're gonna focus this section on block shading so you can get better at shading without even trying. Try to stay in the lines and get a smooth texture in each block. The 2B should be lighter in shade and harder in texture and the 8B should be darker in shade but much softer.

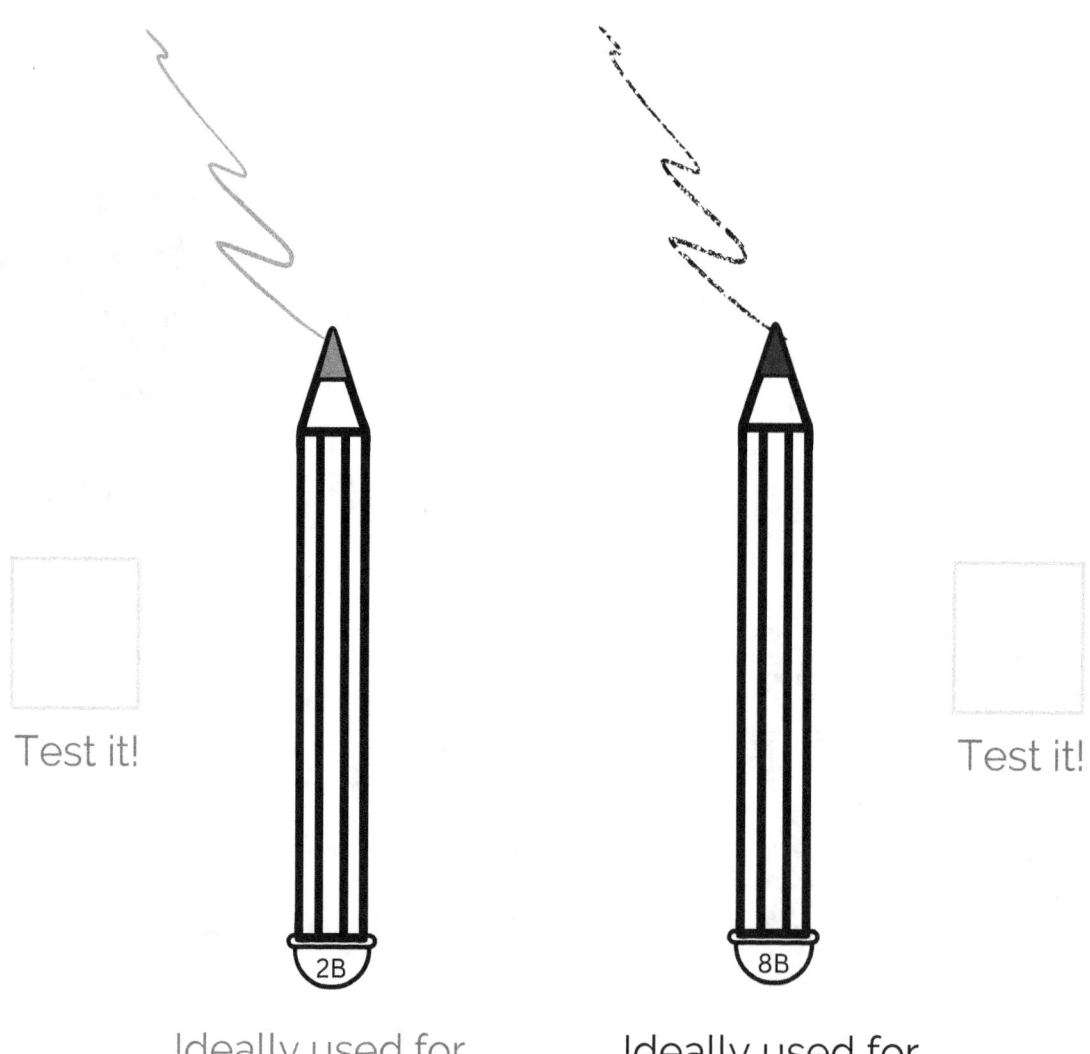

Test it!

Test it!

Ideally used for shades 2-7

Ideally used for shades 5-10

Value Scale

Shade the boxes in evenly to match the scale at the top.
What differences can you see and feel in the pencils?
Tick the boxes to help you remember.

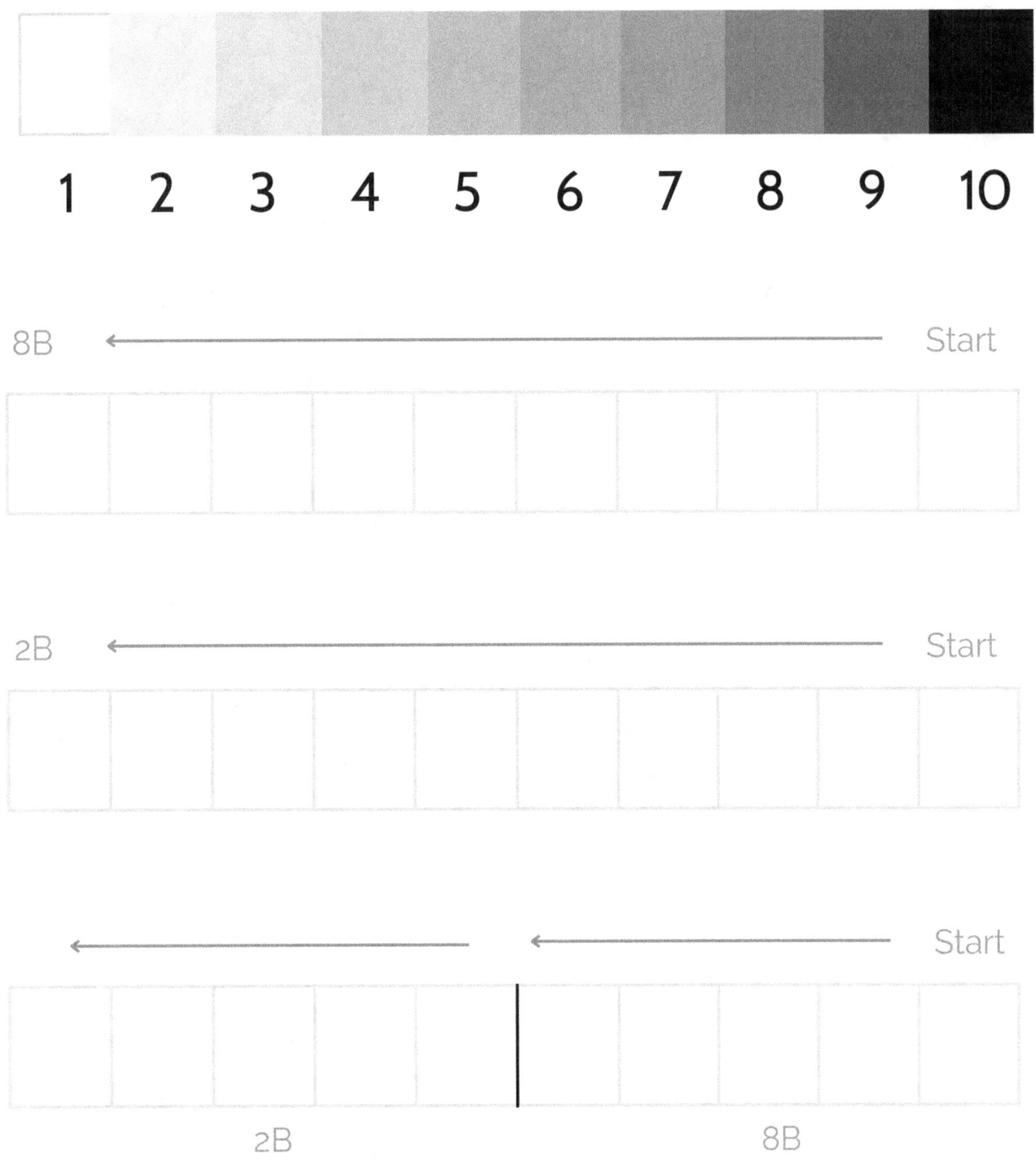

1   2   3   4   5   6   7   8   9   10

8B ⟵——————————————————— Start

2B ⟵——————————————————— Start

⟵—————————— ⟵—————————— Start

2B   8B

13

Make the white boxes disappear.

Make the white boxes match the outer shade.

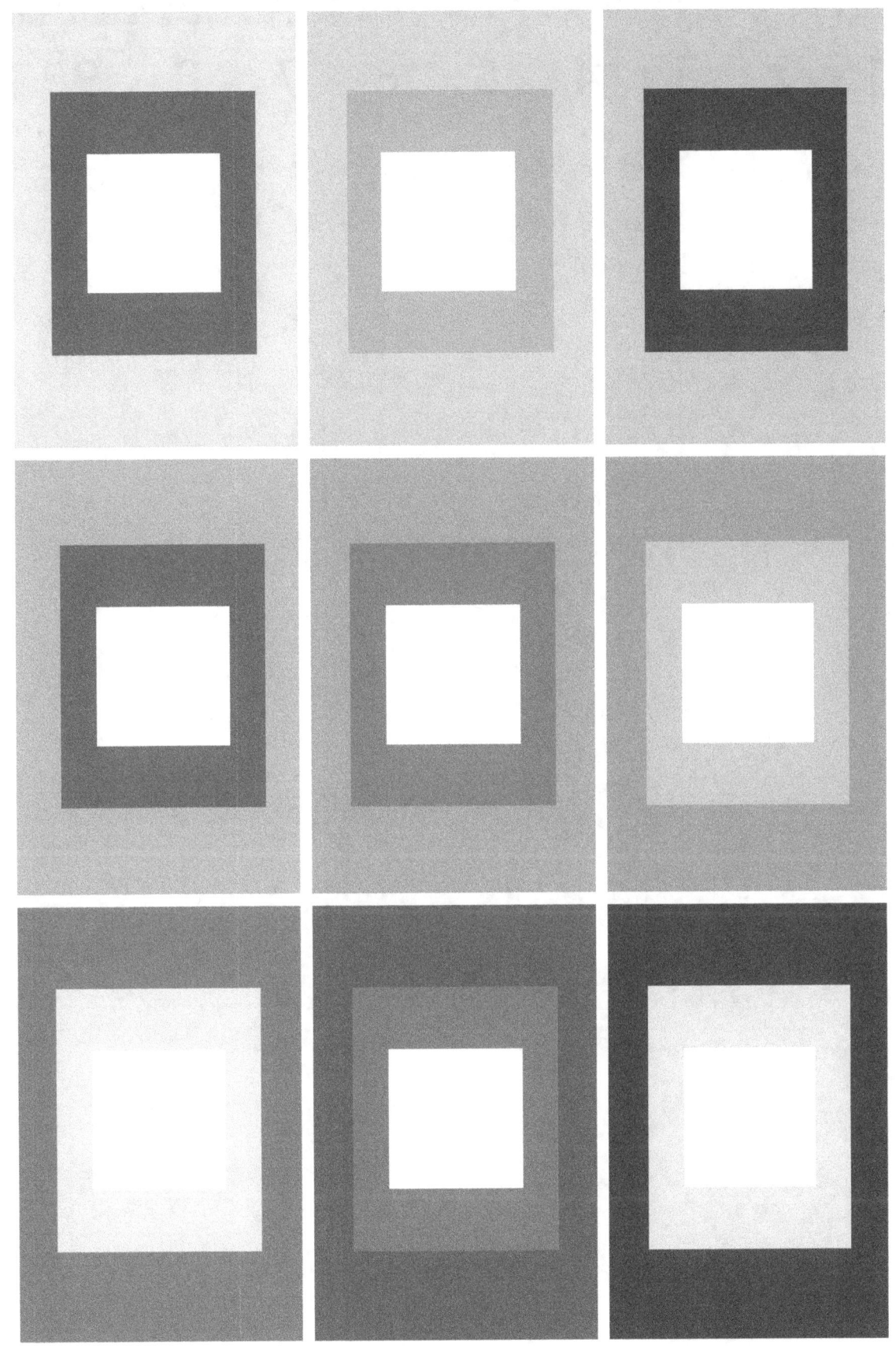

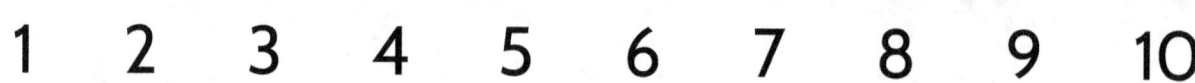

Shade the face in the right shade to match the number on the scale.

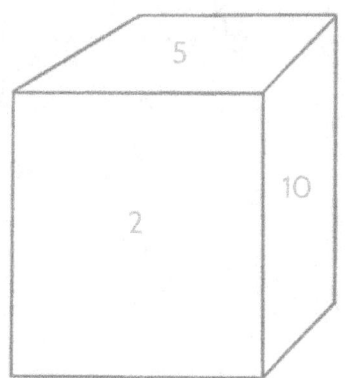

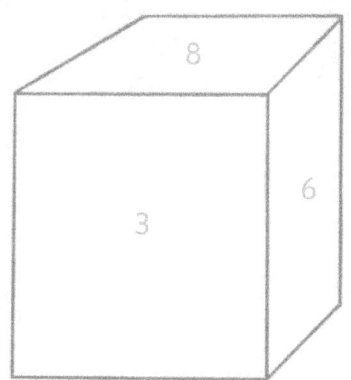

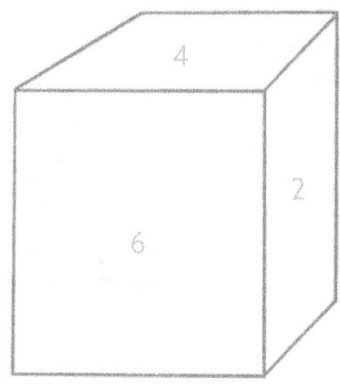

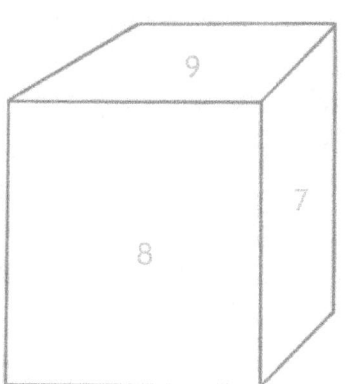

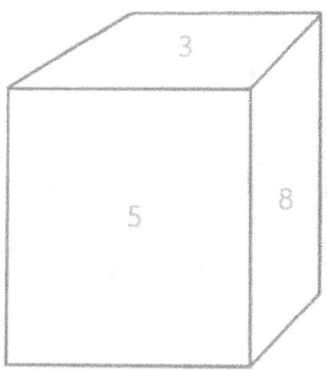

16

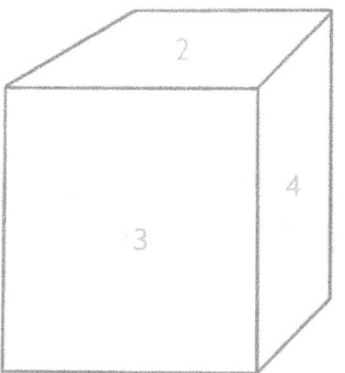

Decide which numbers you want to use to shade
in the text, just like we did with the squares.

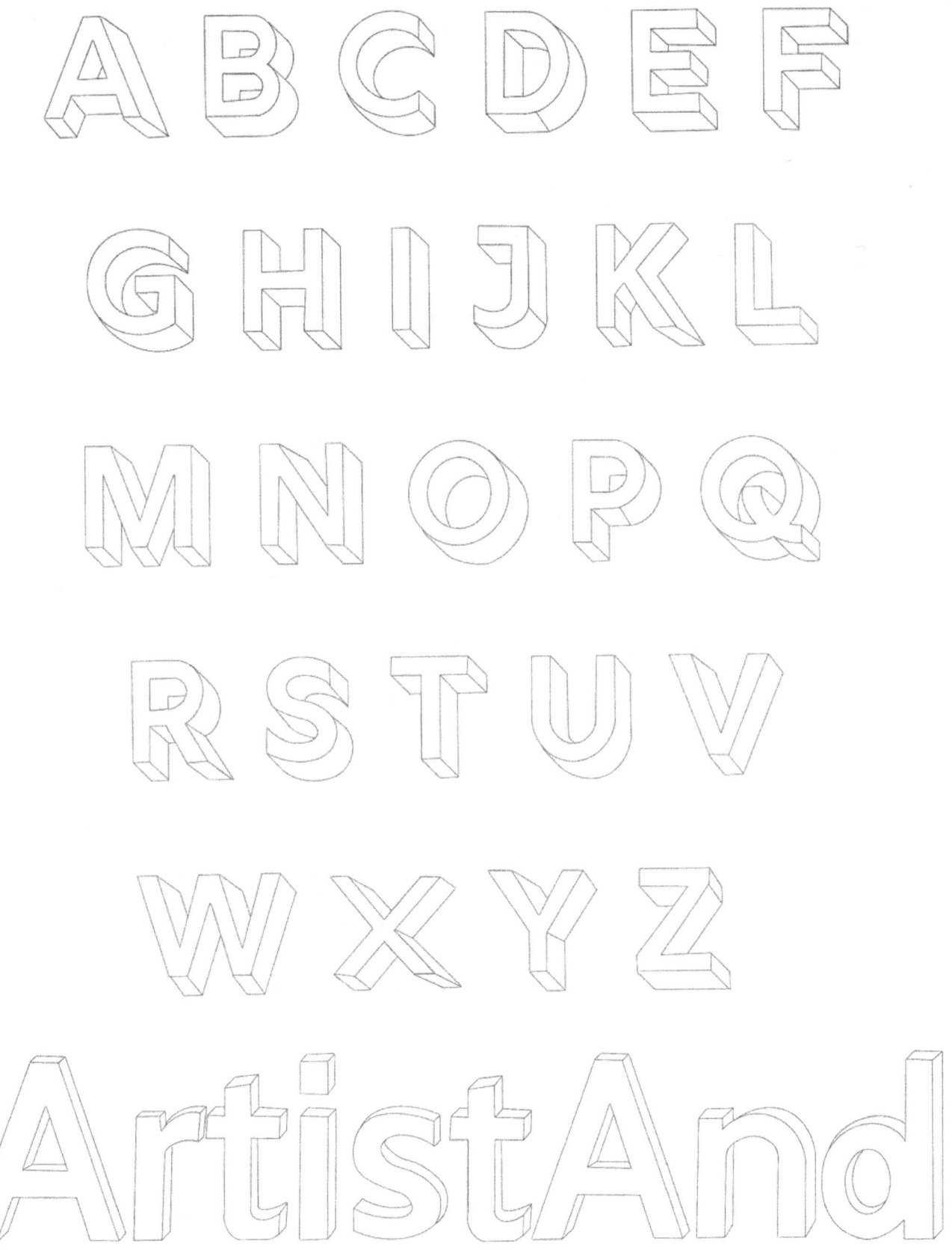

If you roll a pencil down
   a hill, is it stationery?

3D Shading In Blocks

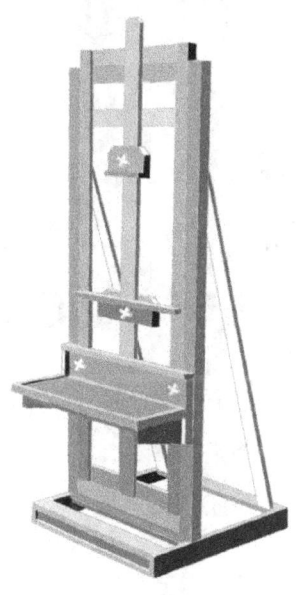

Use the value scale at the tops of the pages to match the numbers on your drawing. Those view finders might be a good idea now. You can put one on the reference pic, and one on the value scale to see if the values match. Then you can put one on your piece and one on the reference pic to check you're matching up too! Try to have your shading as smooth as possible for the best results.

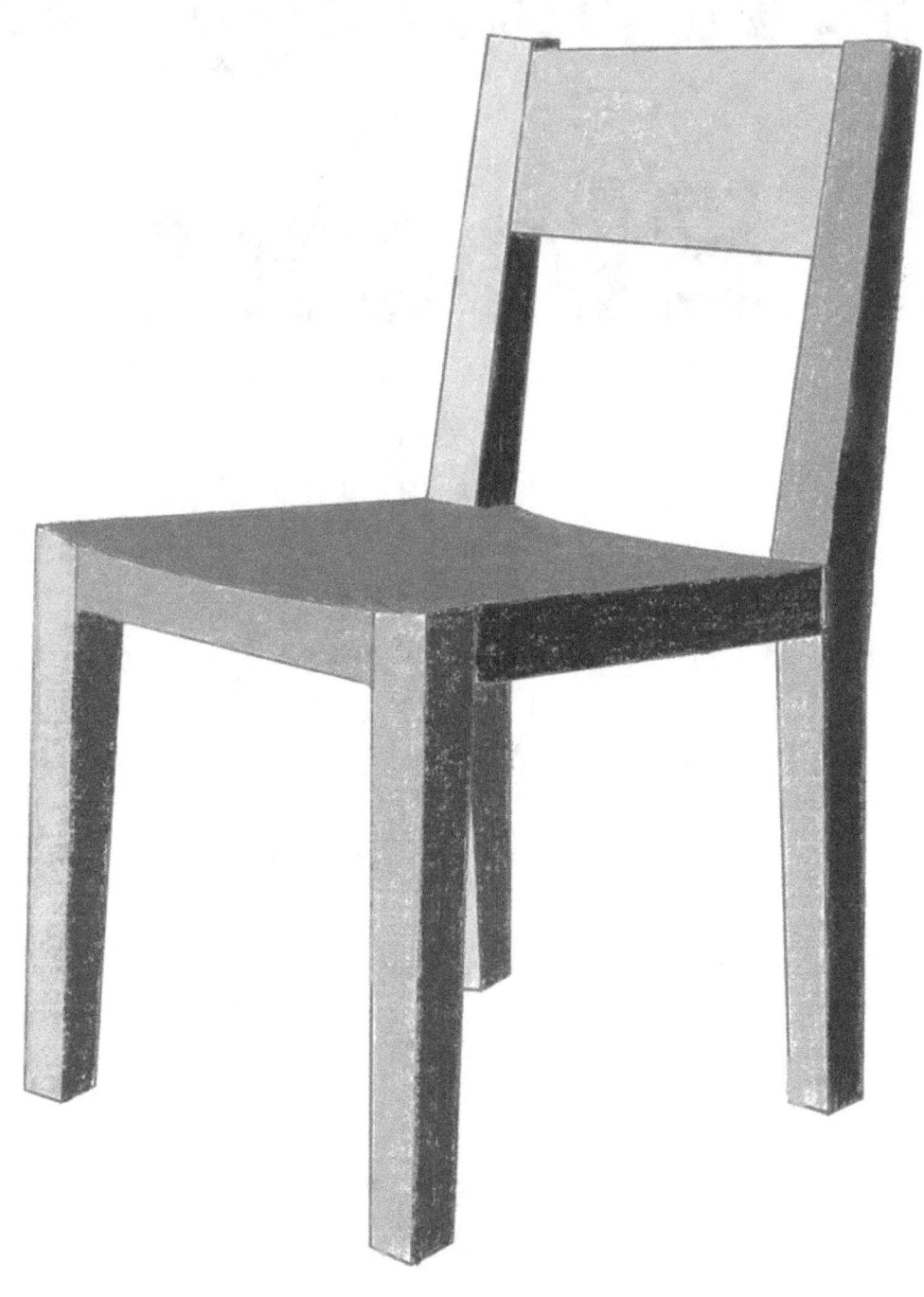

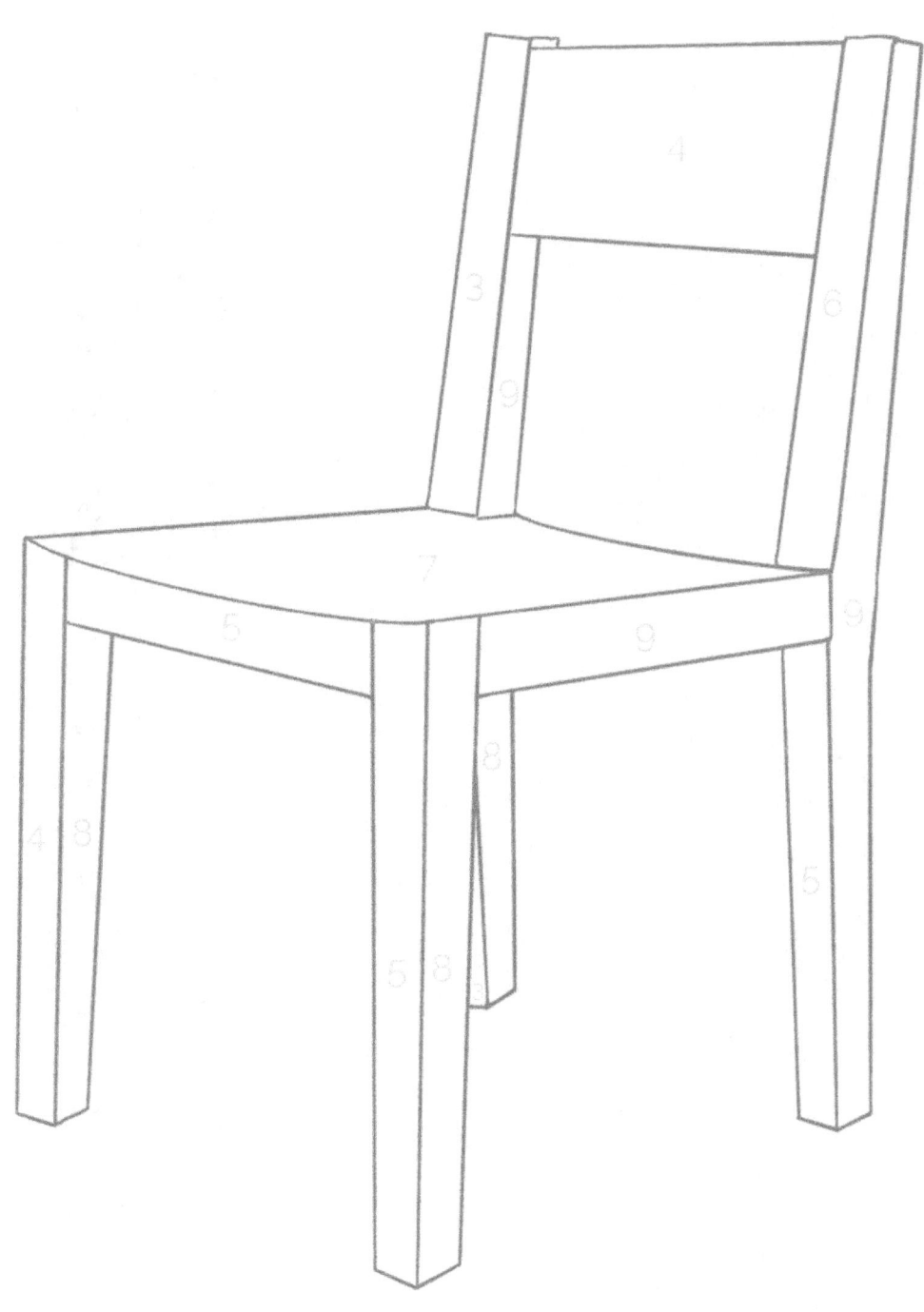

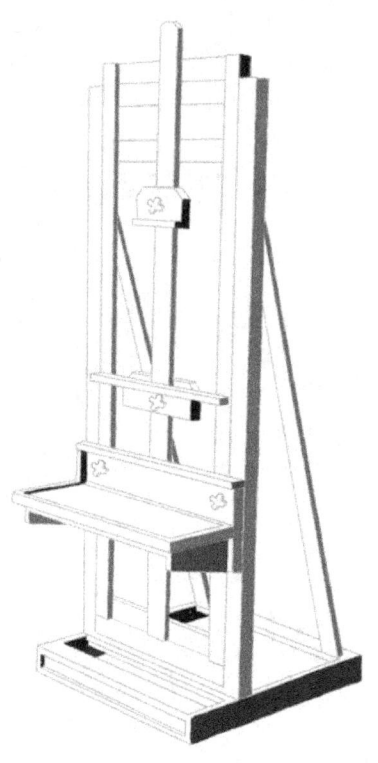

Right Face

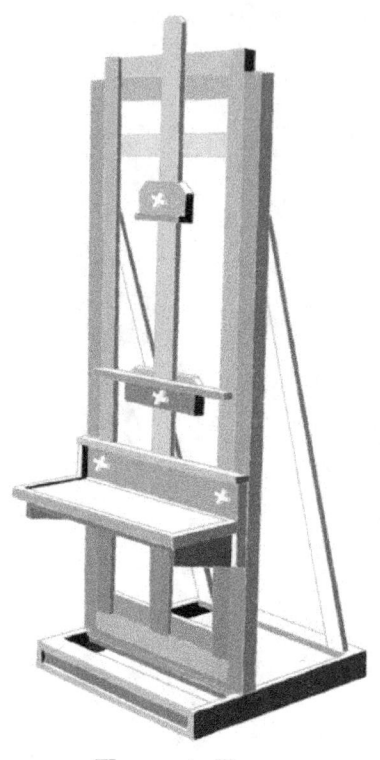

Front Face

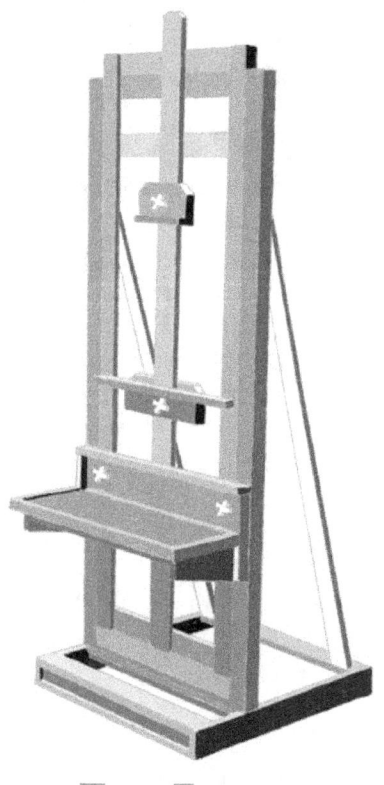

Top Face

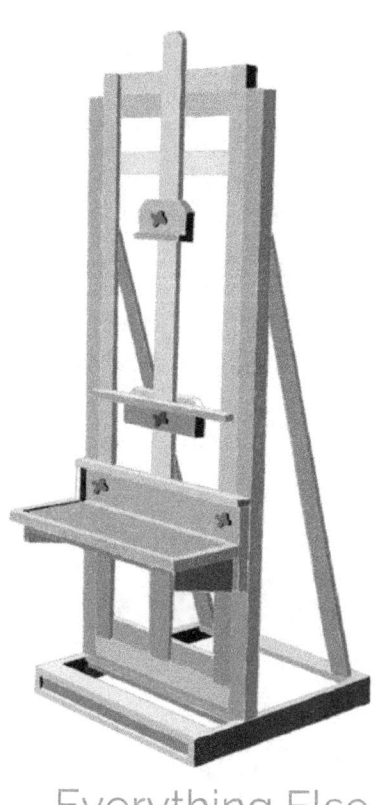

Everything Else

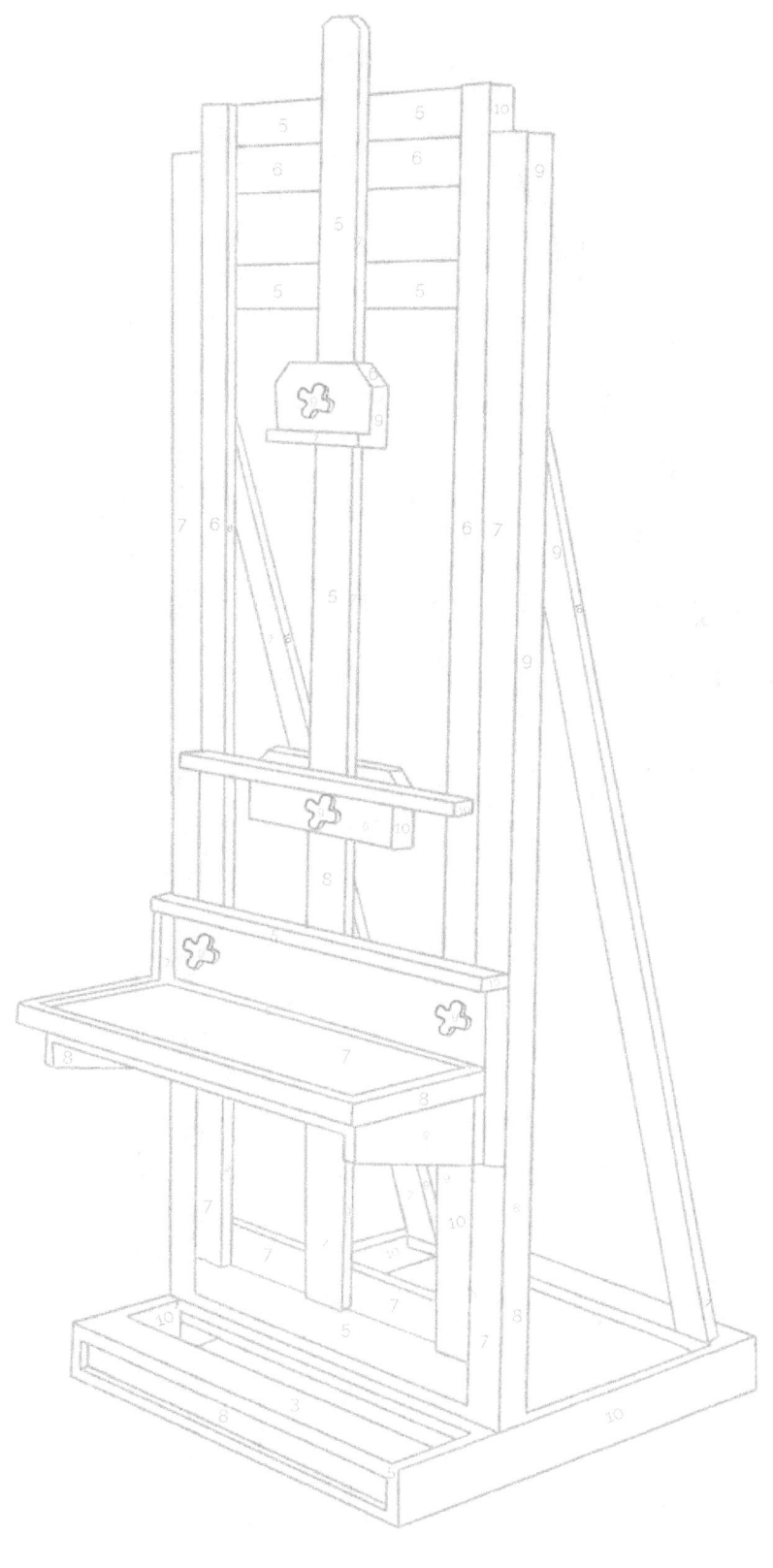

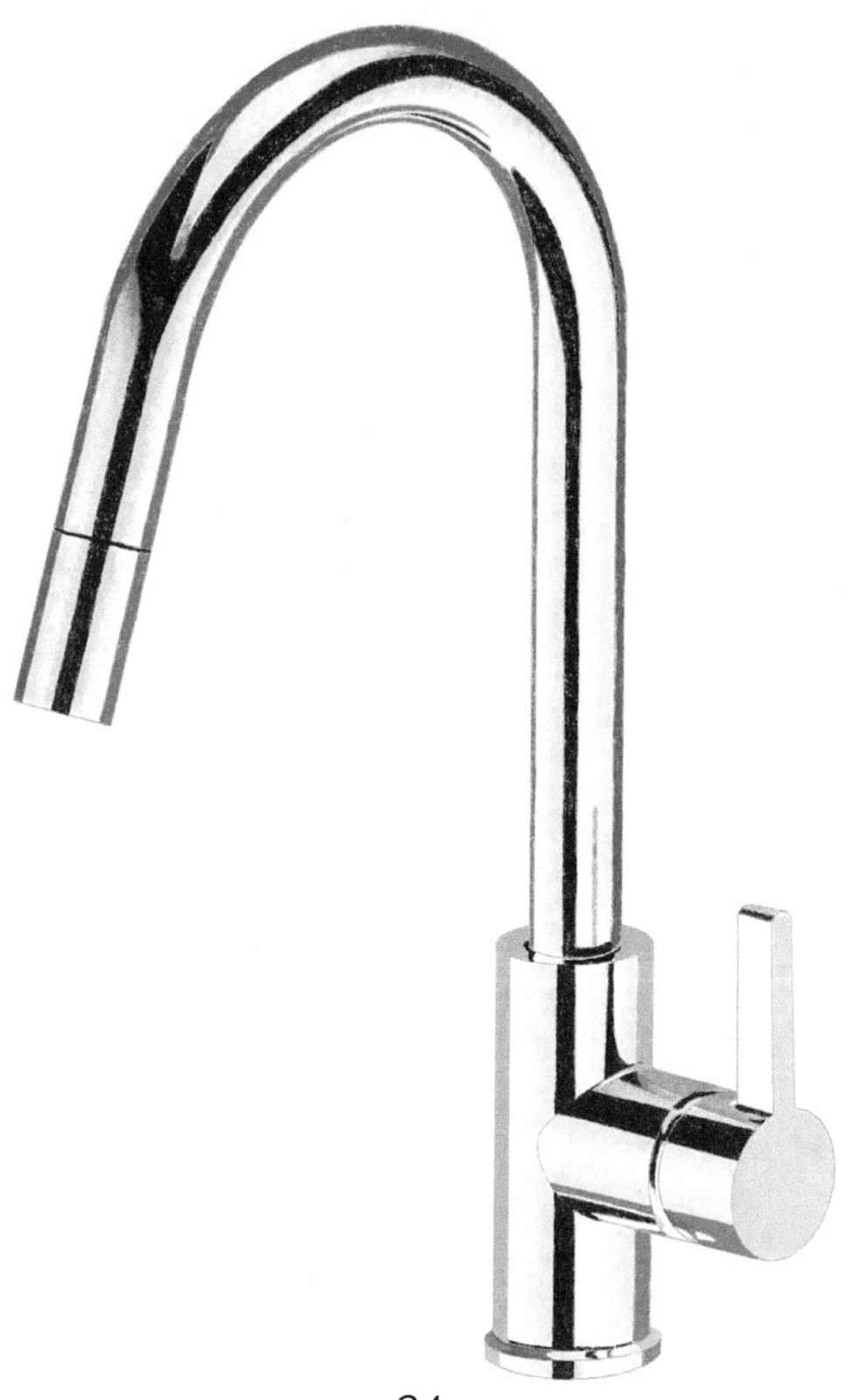

24

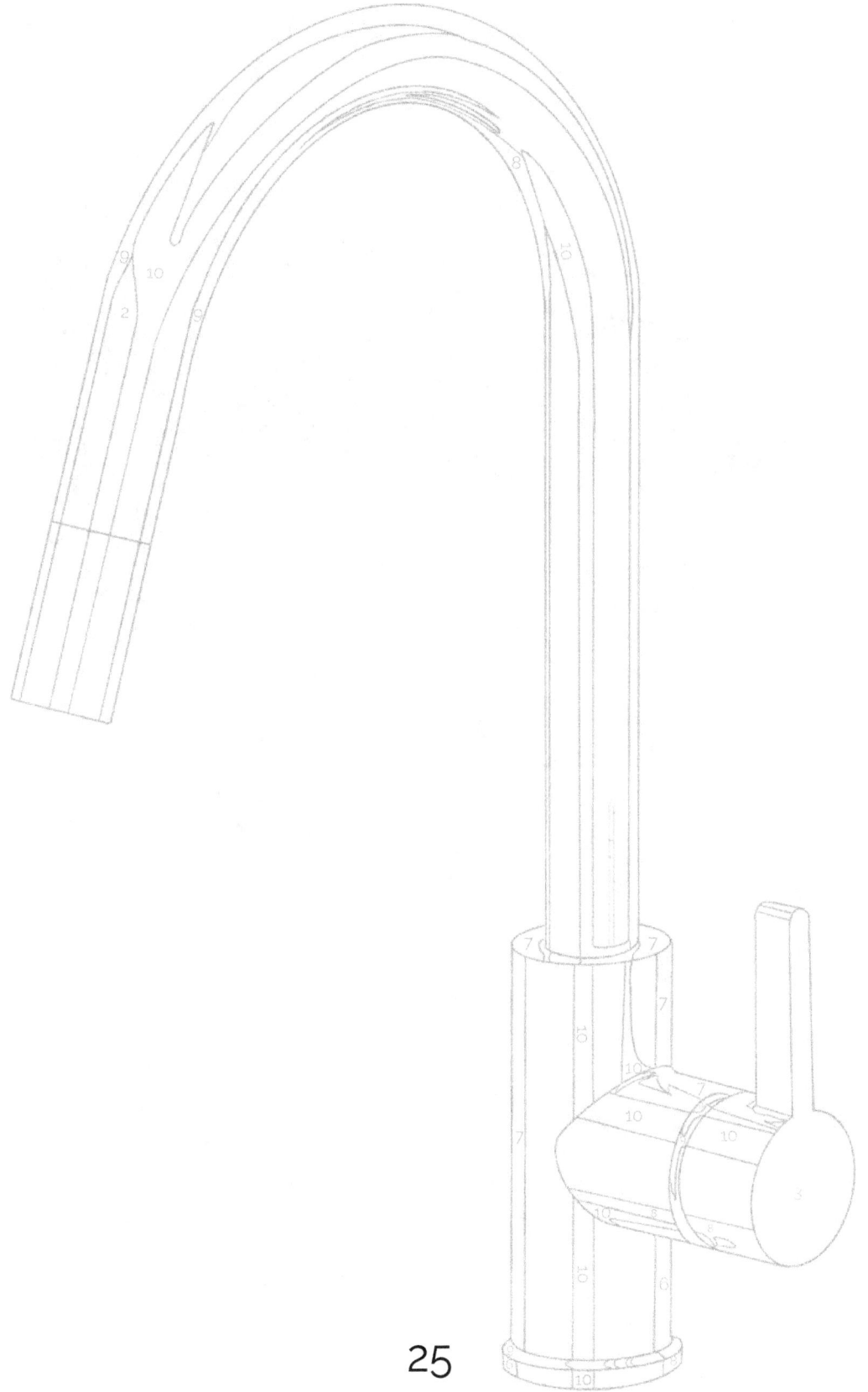

1 2 3 4 5 6 7 8 9 10

25

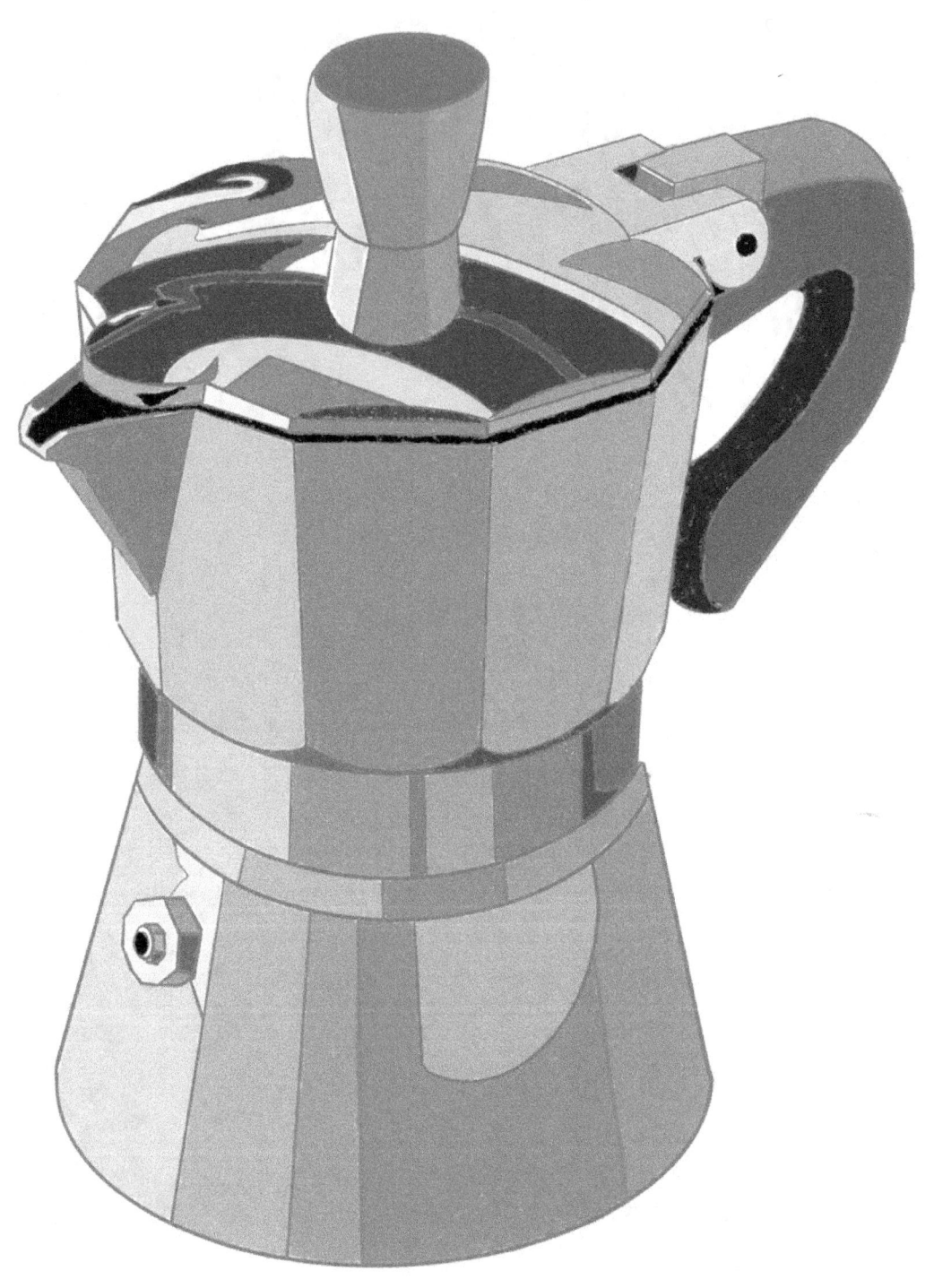

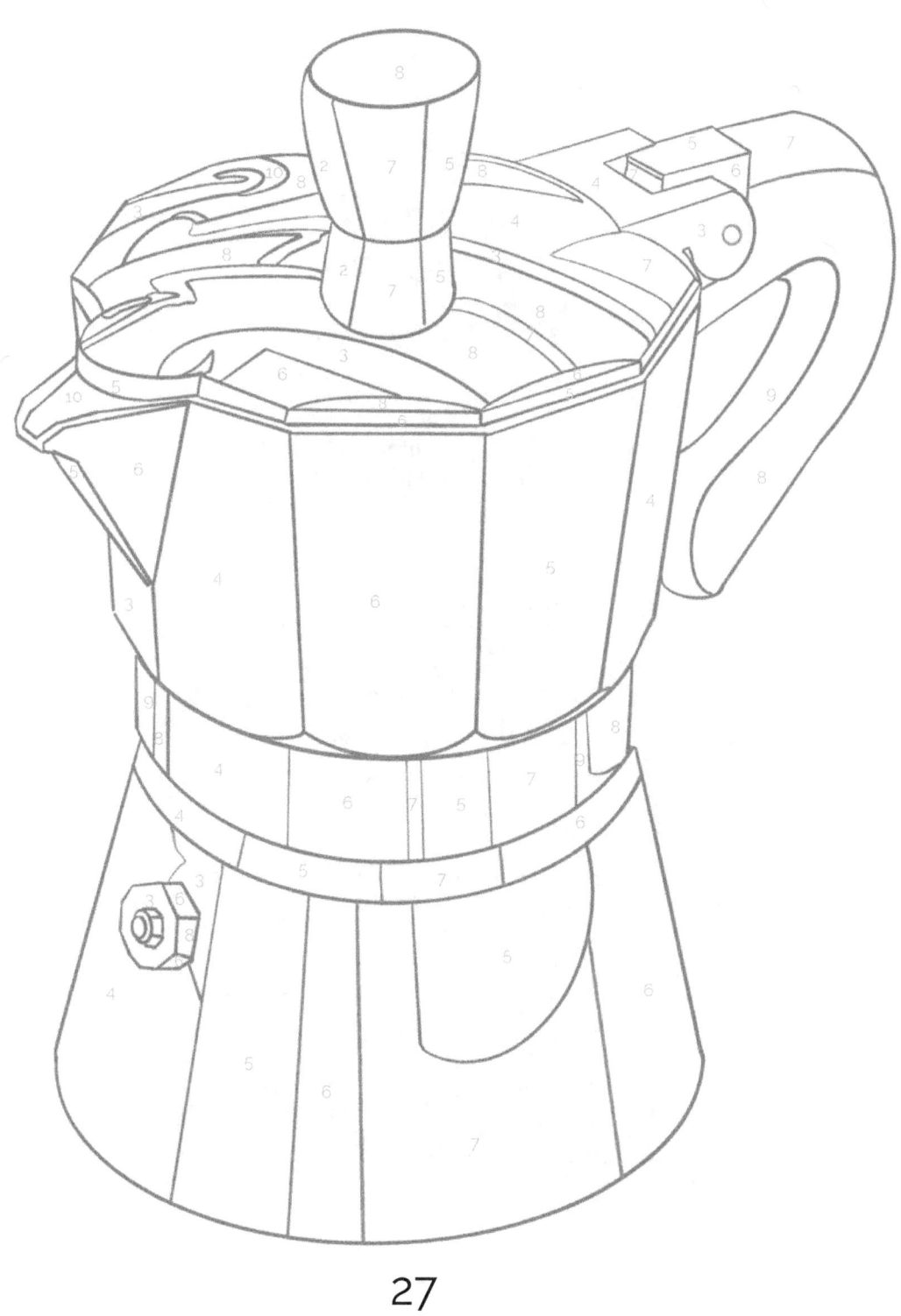

Try it without the numbers for
this one. See if you can match
the shades from the picture!

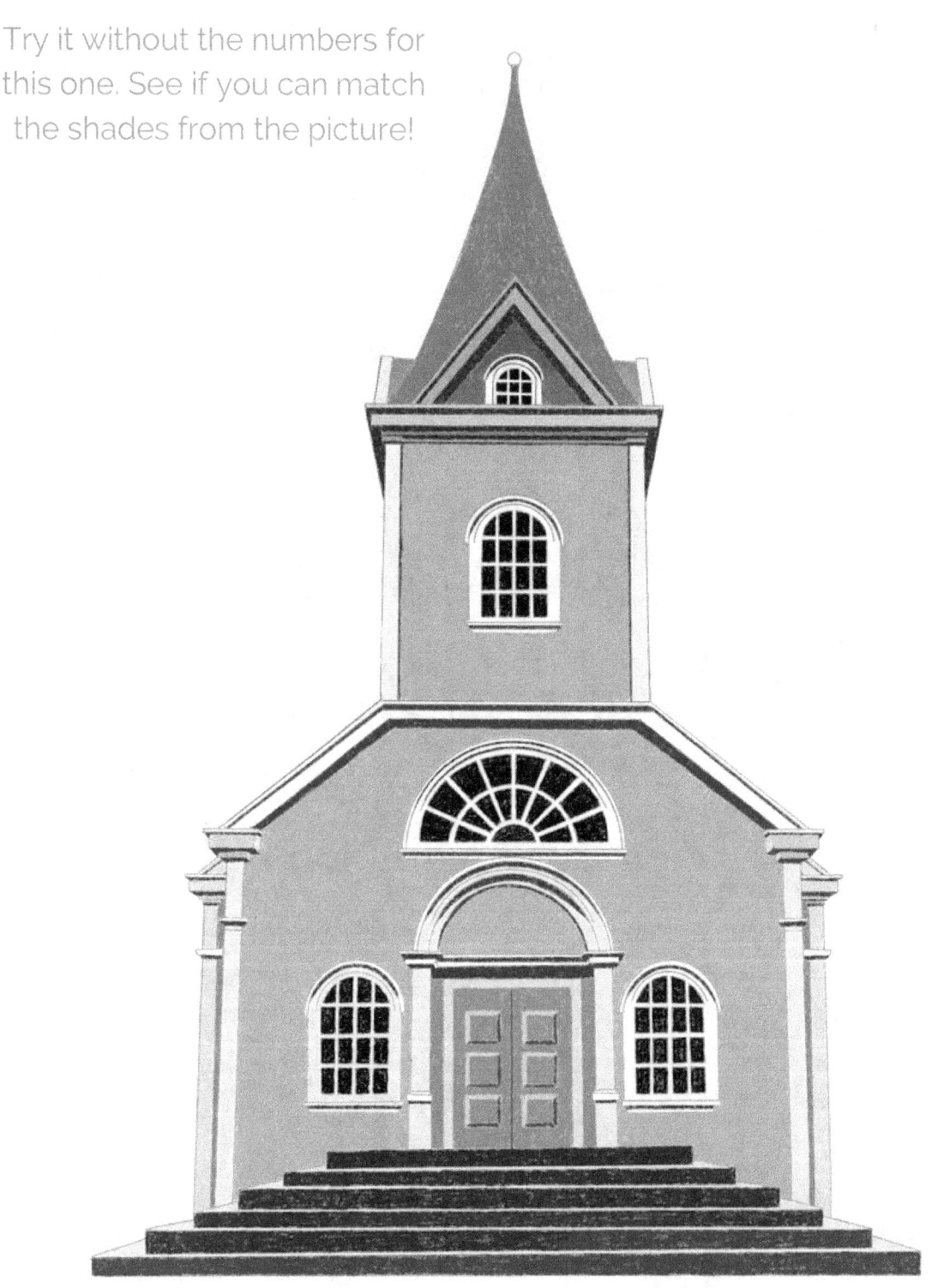

1 2 3 4 5 6 7 8 9 10

29

Broken pencils are
pointless.

Gradients

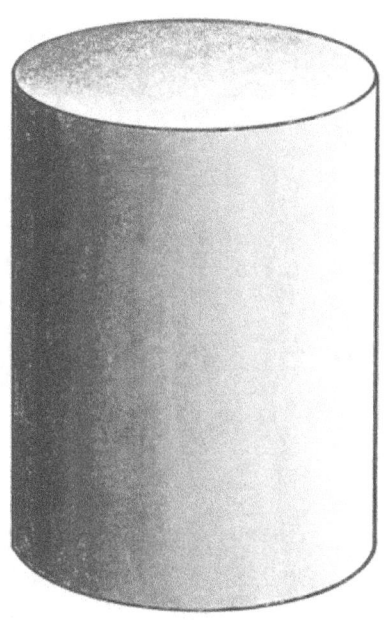

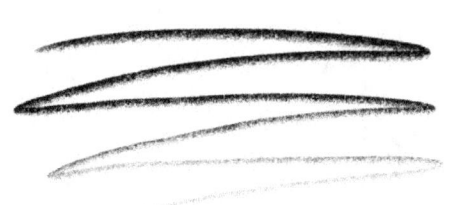

Gradients are what give objects and illusion of being curved. Without gradients everything can look quite flat and that's not what we're after! Practise these exercises on the next few pages and see how curved you can make your objects look with the gradients. Make sure you have lots of ranges of shade!

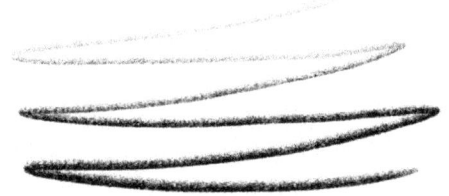

Gradient Scale

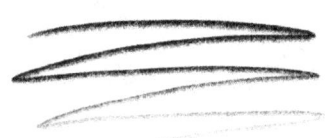

Copy this gradient scale using your different pencils below:

8B ← Start

2B ← Start

← ← Start

2B 8B

Blending Edges

1. Choose one of the boxes below or draw your own

2. Shade one dark, one light. It doesn't matter which is which.

3. Only shade in the lighter box, don't go over the darker one or else you'll get a thick dark line.

Blend in this space

4. Gently apply pressure until you match the dark shade and pull the gradient into the lighter section

Try a few different shades here and see if you can blend in the edges!

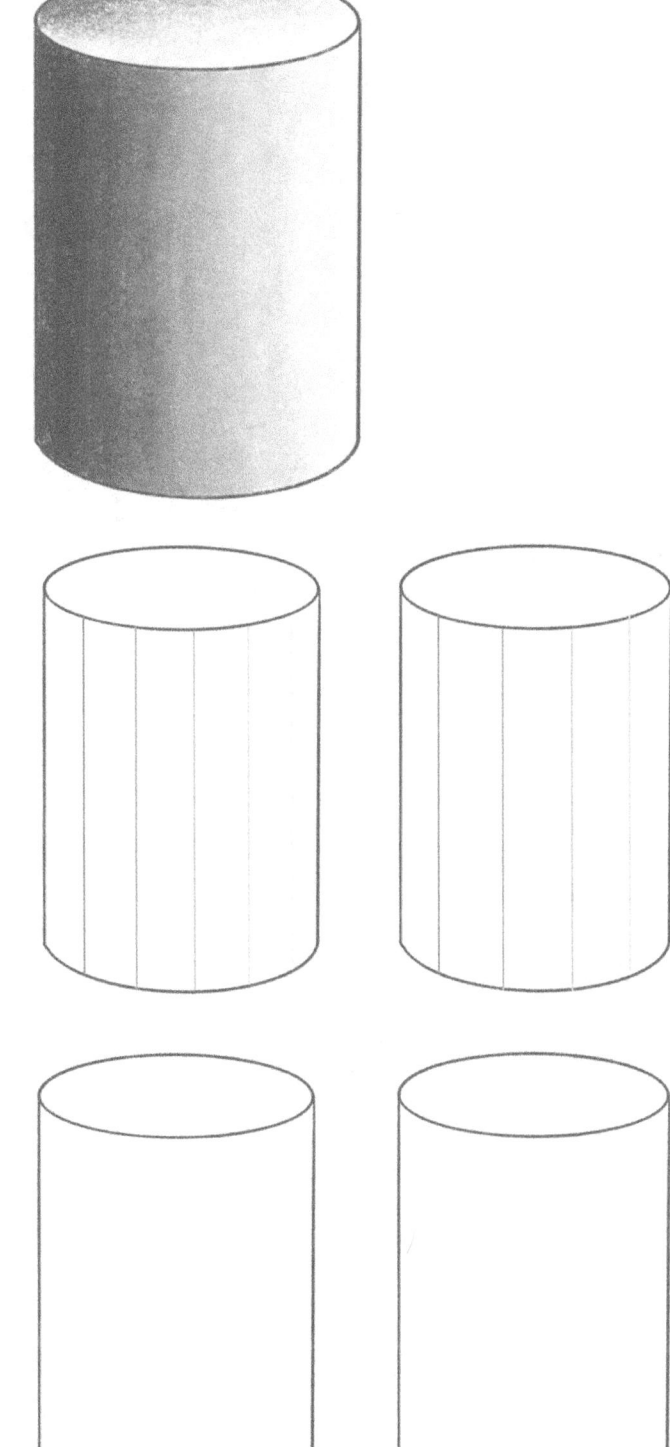

Try these gradients using solid blocks from the beginning of the book and blending like we just did.

10

8

6

4

I failed my art exam using
the wrong pencil...I guess it
wasn't 2b.

3D
Blending

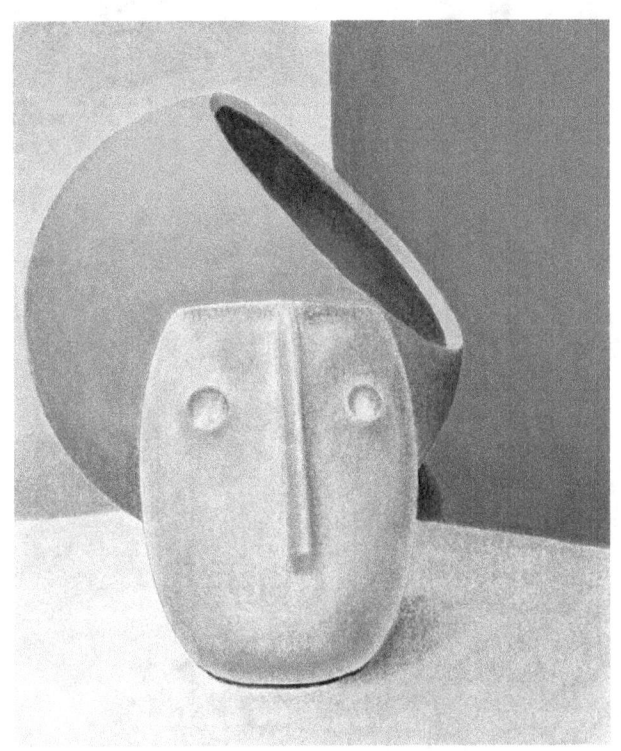

Now you're a pro, and you can go from hard edges to soft edges, you're ready to embark on a shading journey like no other. This is the stuff that makes things look even more 3D and curved. For many of these drawings, you can add a base block layer like before and then add a gradient on top! Or, if you want to go hardcore, see if you can go straight in with a gradient.

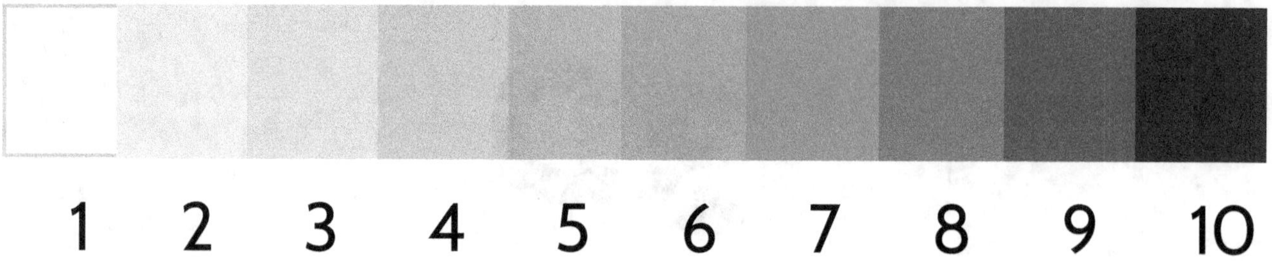
1 2 3 4 5 6 7 8 9 10

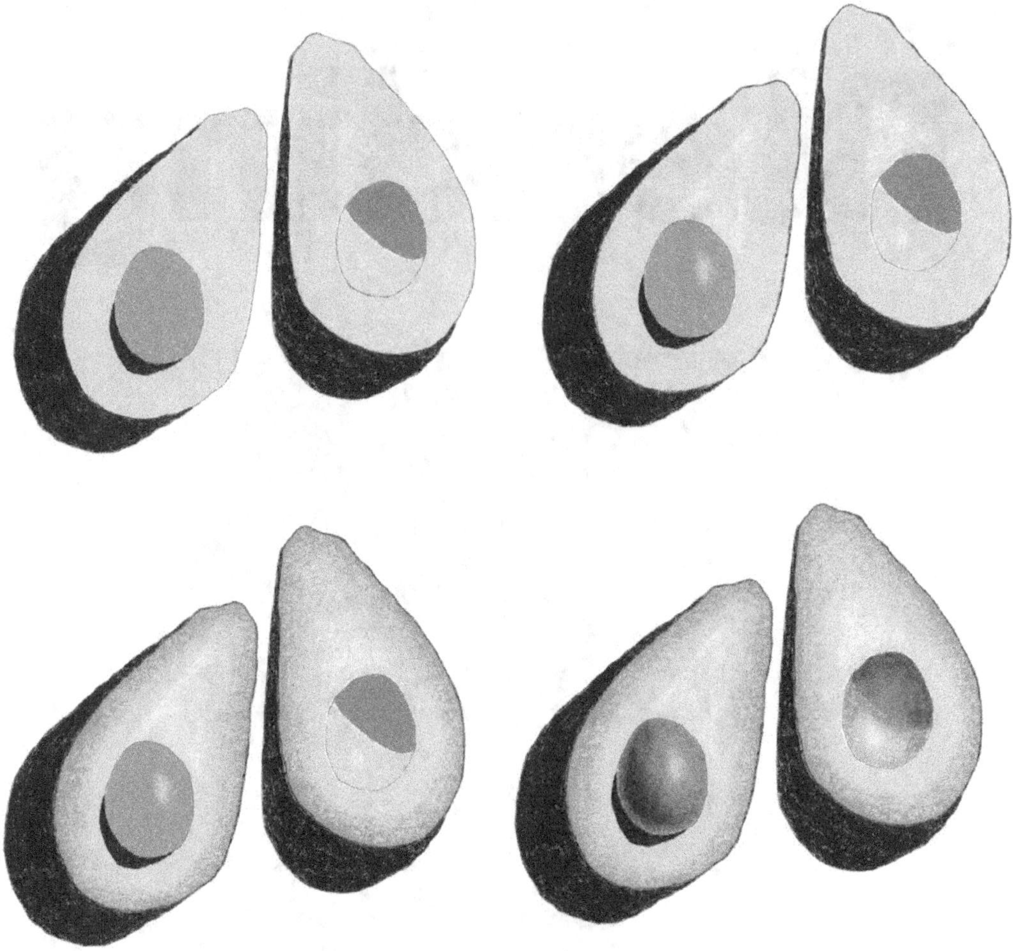

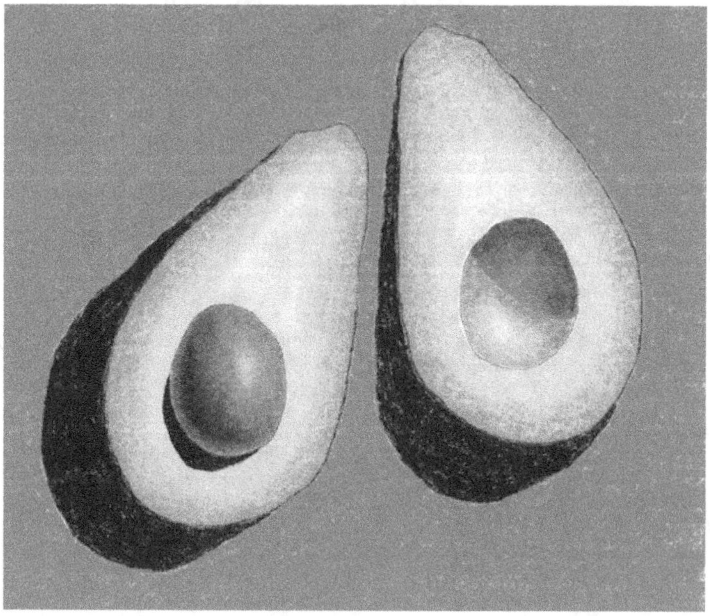

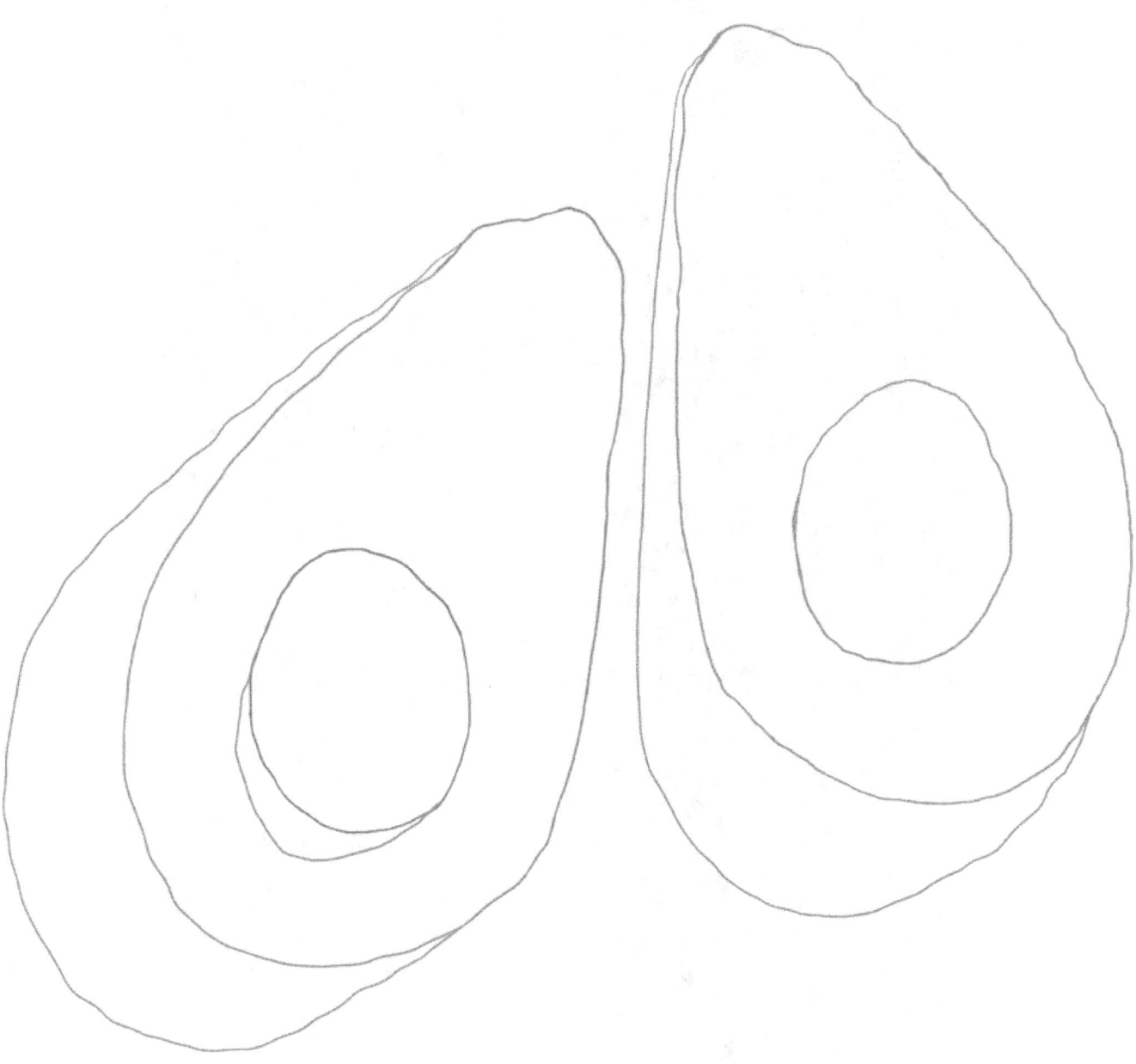

1 2 3 4 5 6 7 8 9 10

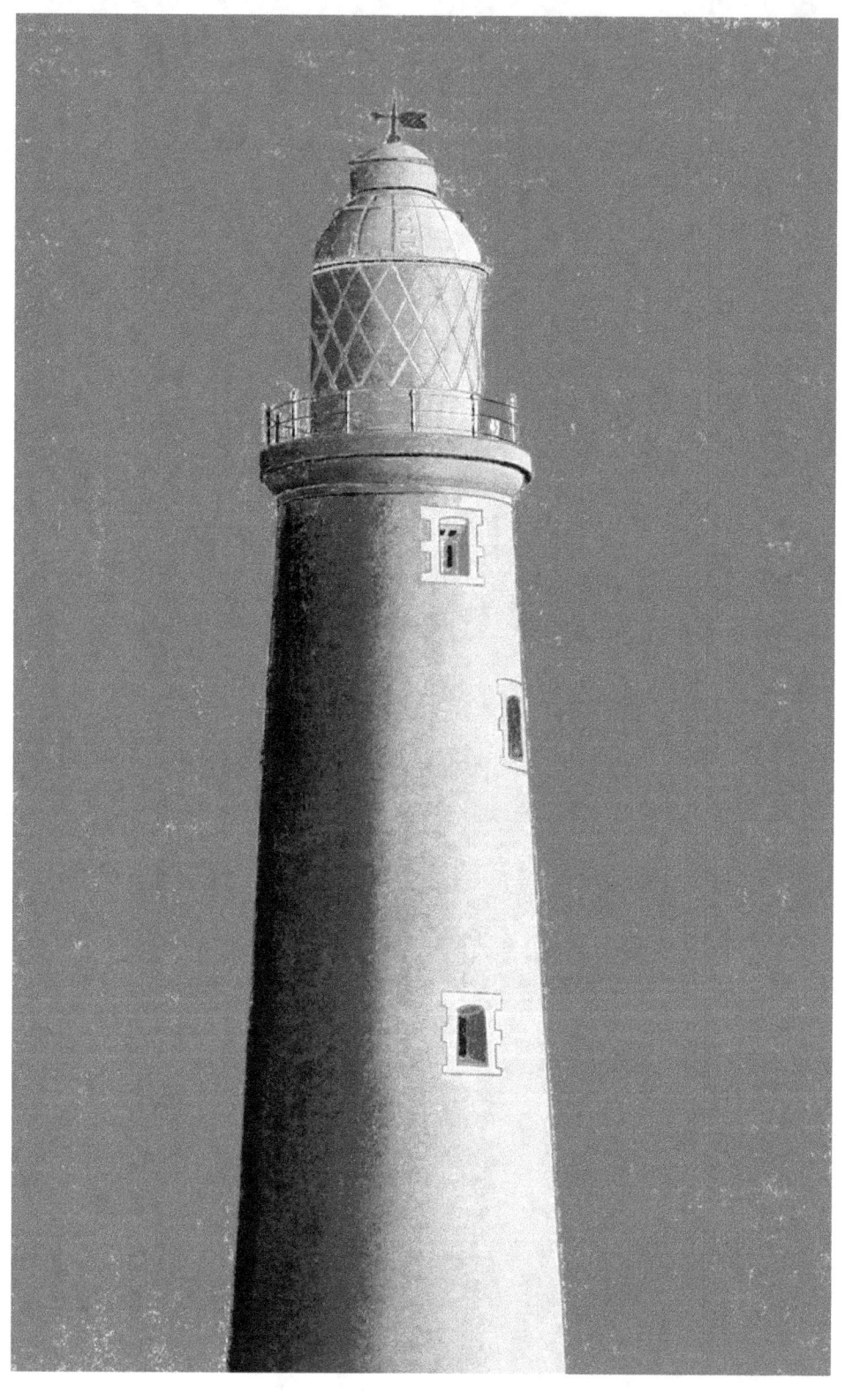

1 2 3 4 5 6 7 8 9 10

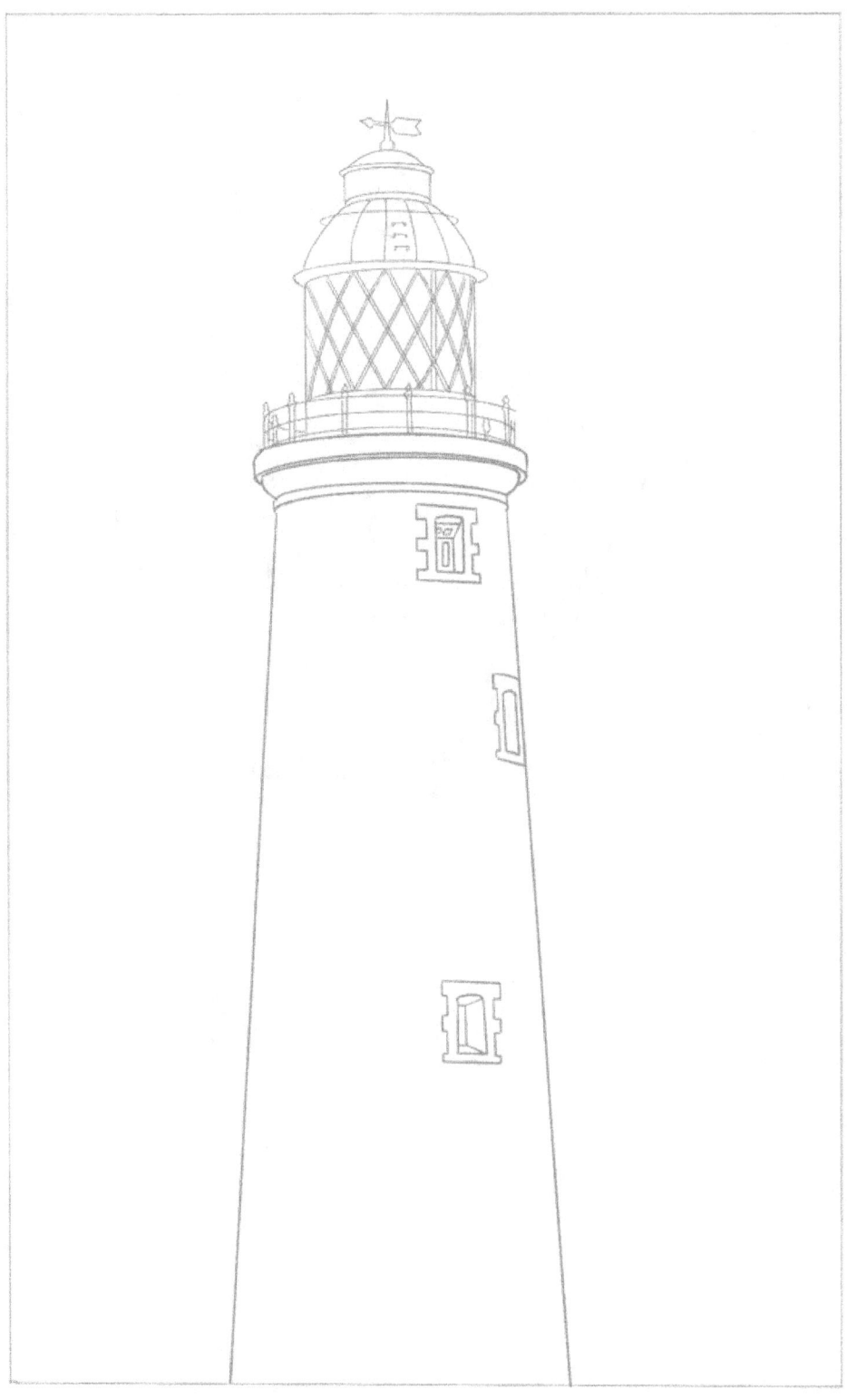

1 2 3 4 5 6 7 8 9 10

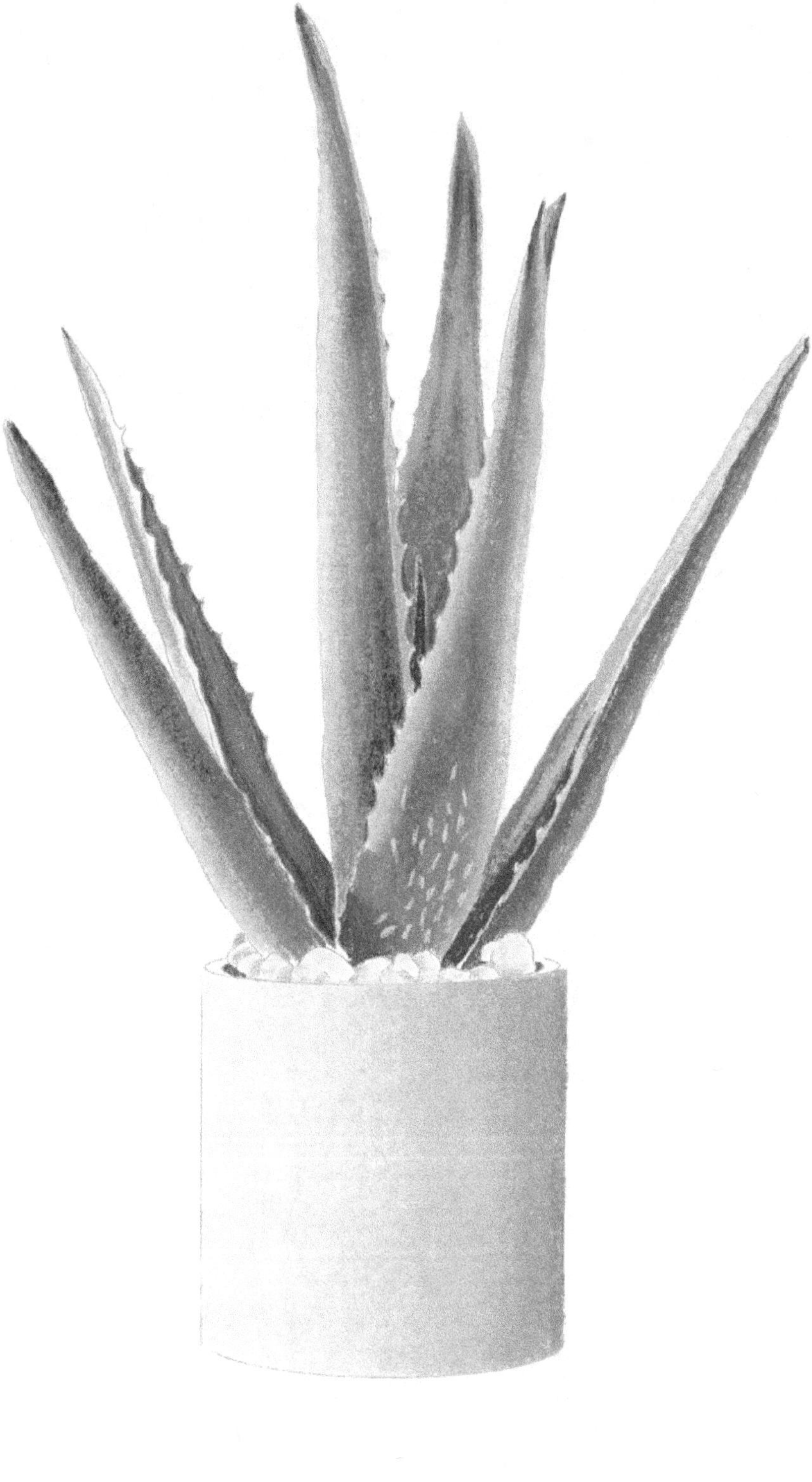

43

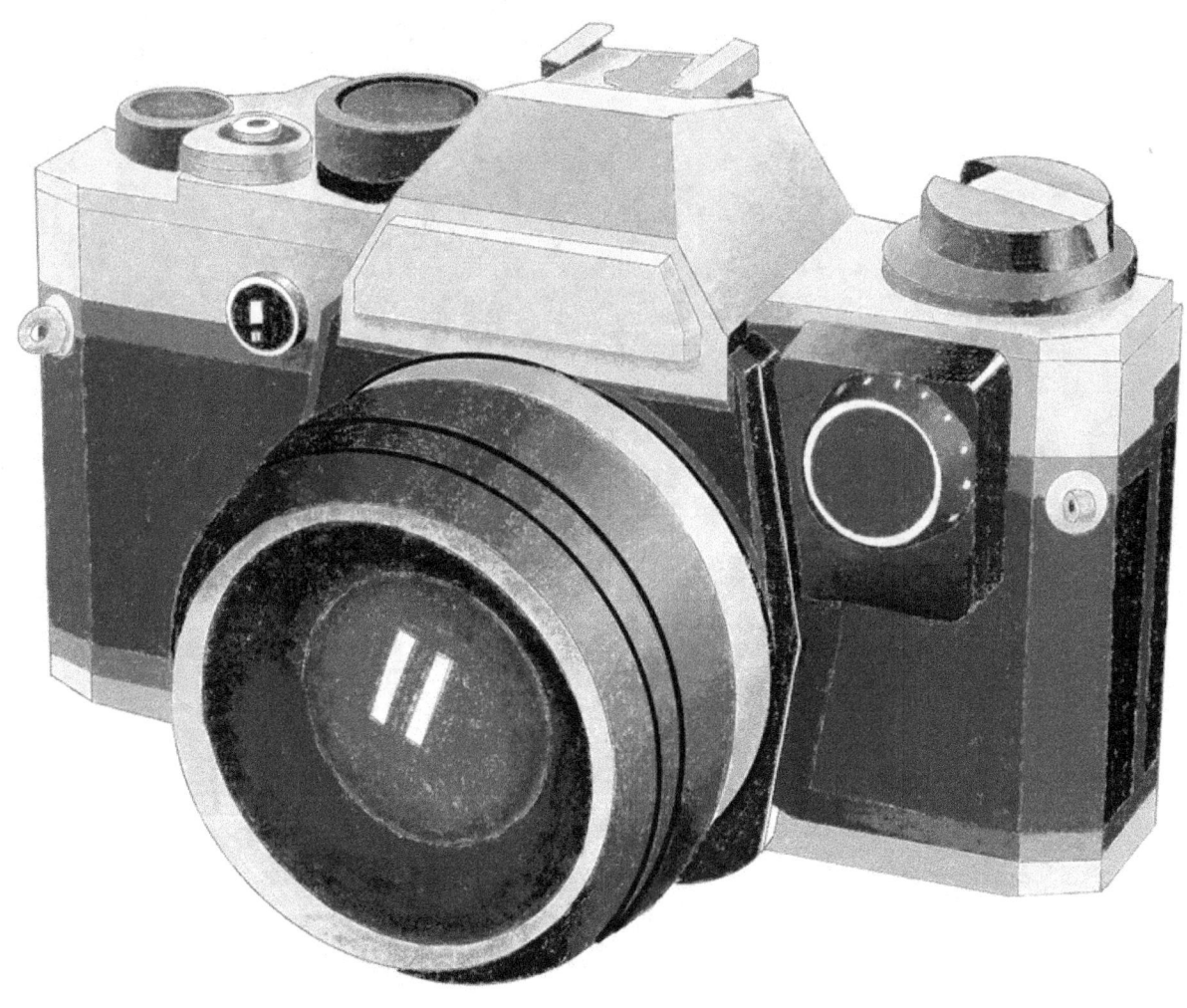

1 2 3 4 5 6 7 8 9 10

1   2   3   4   5   6   7   8   9   10

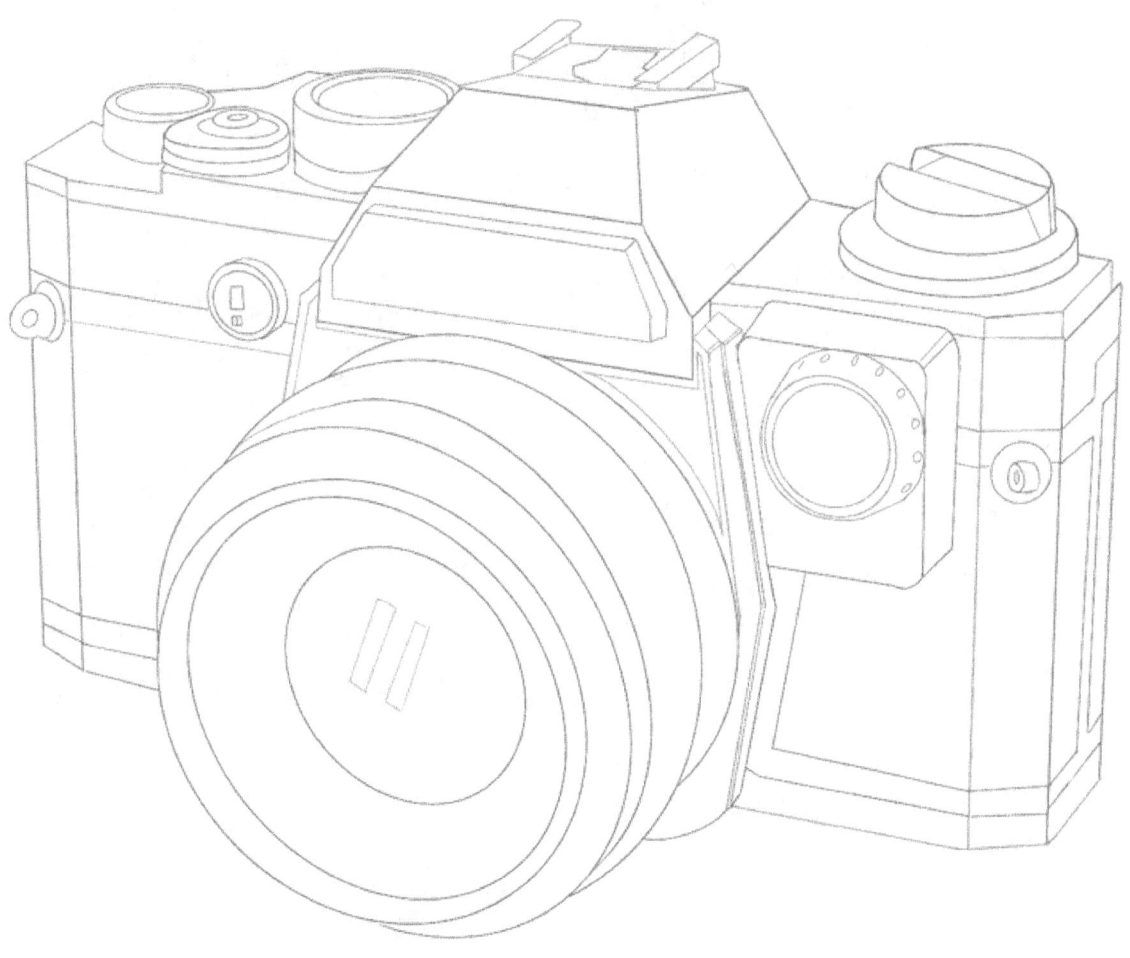

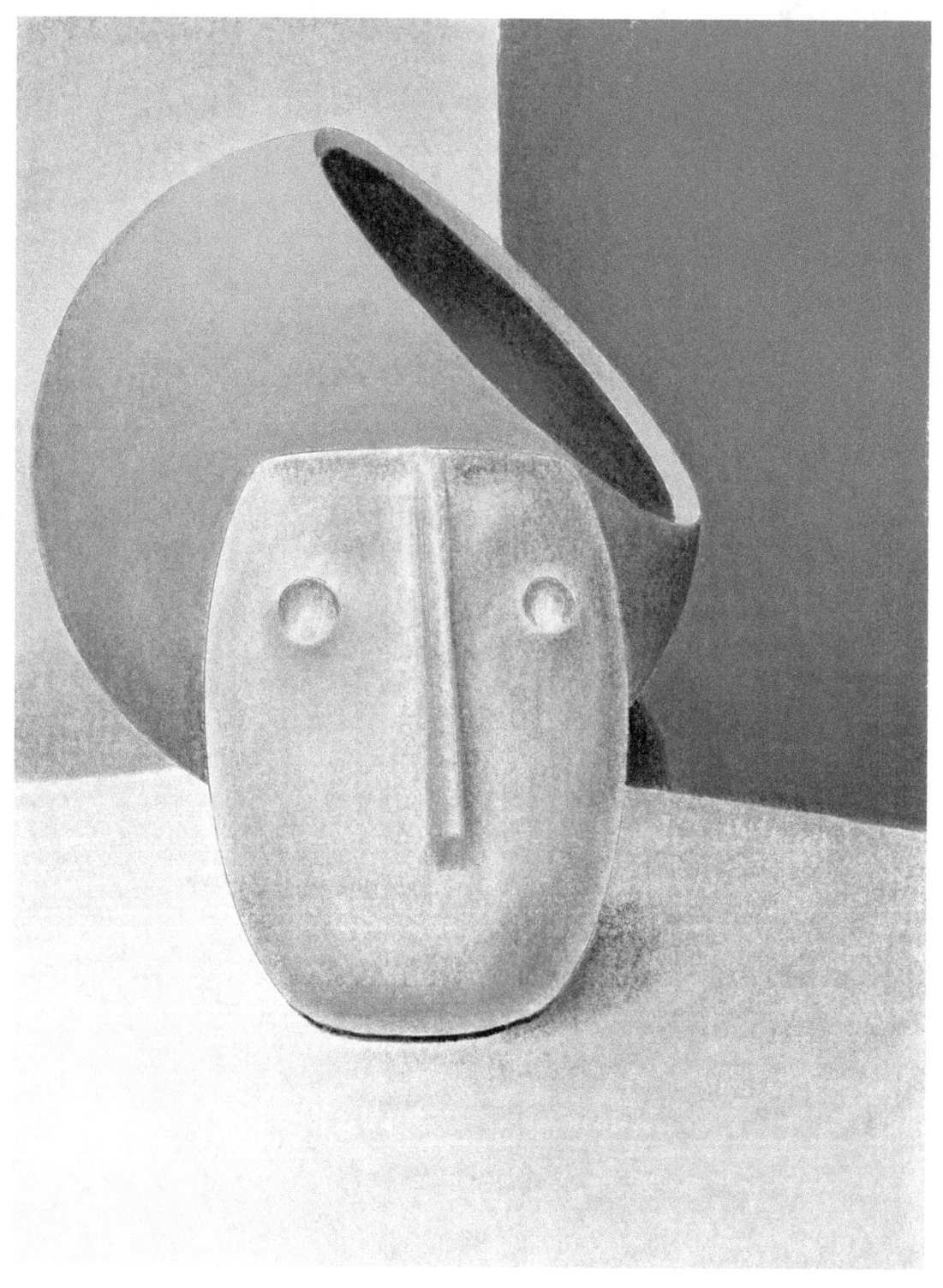

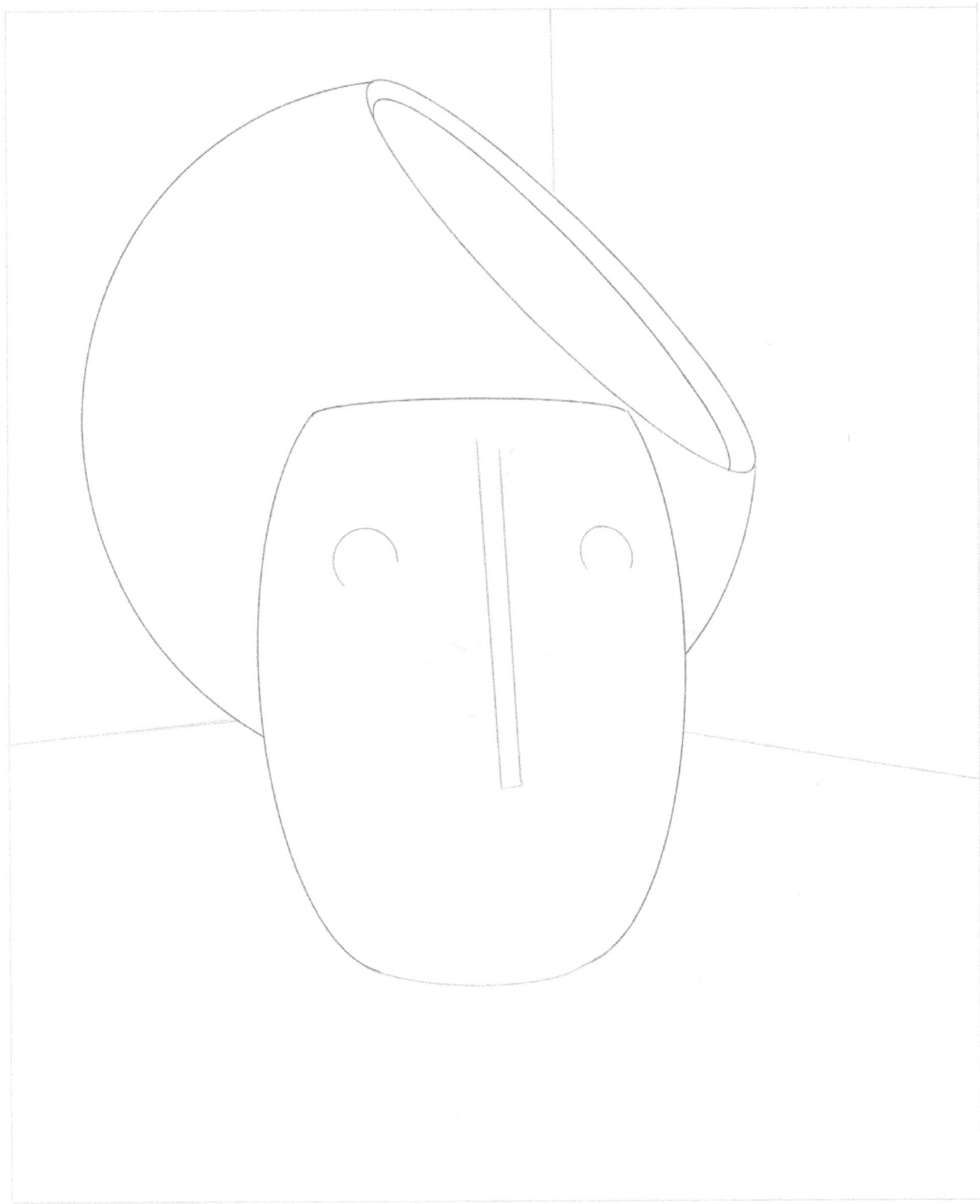

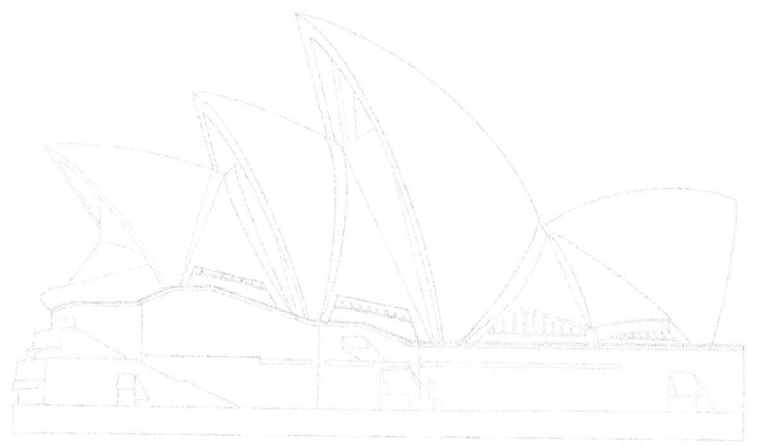

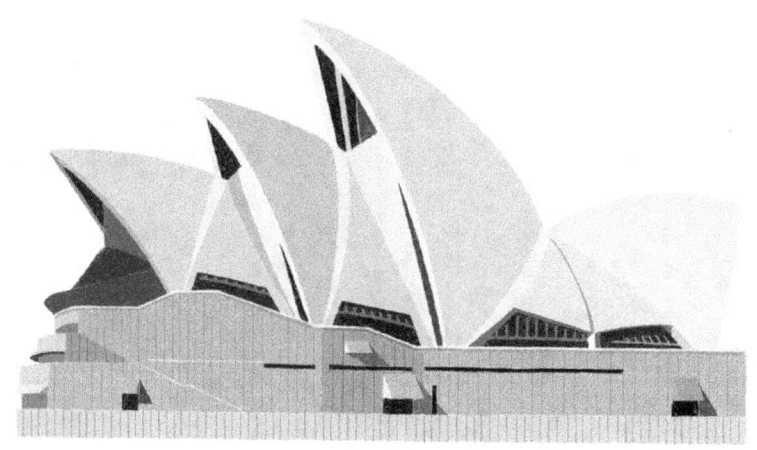

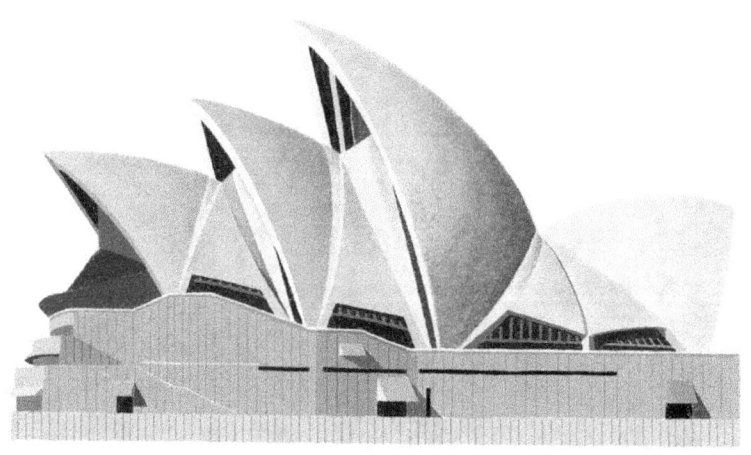

48

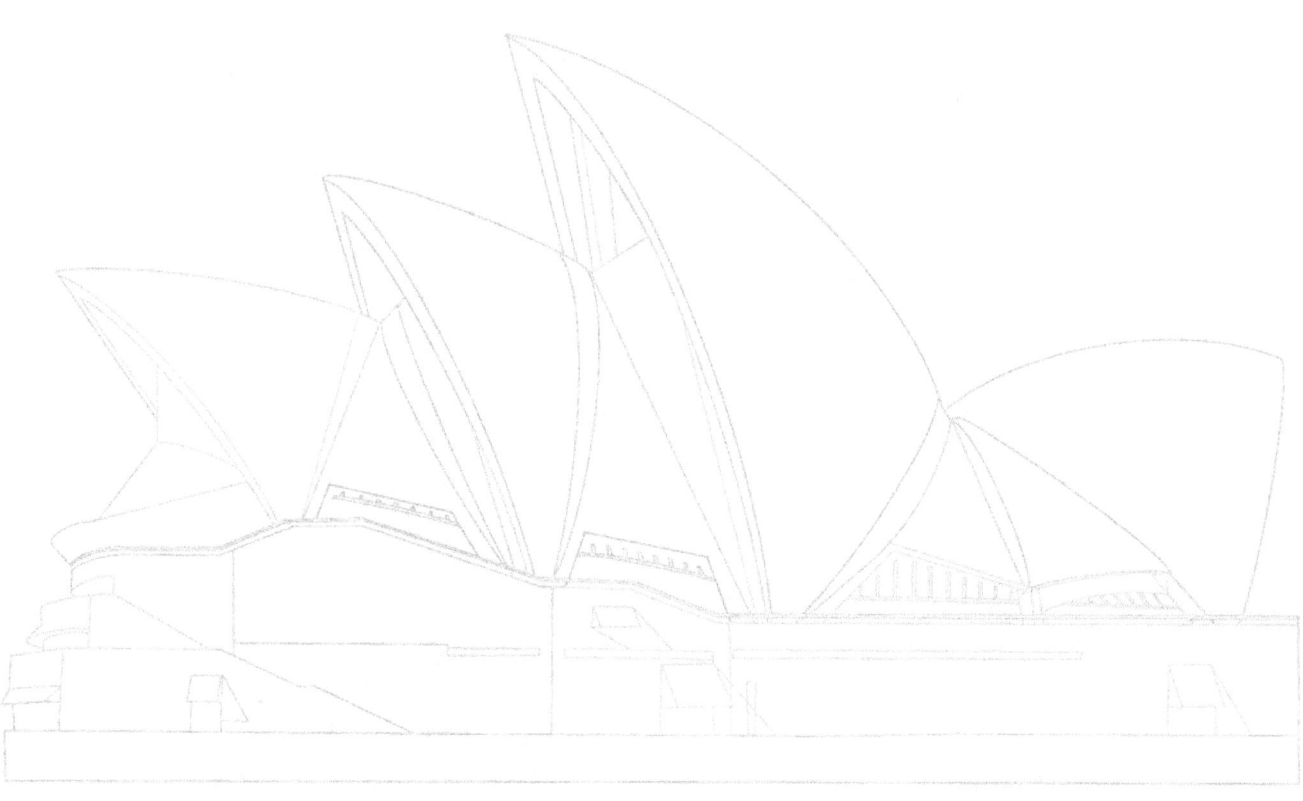

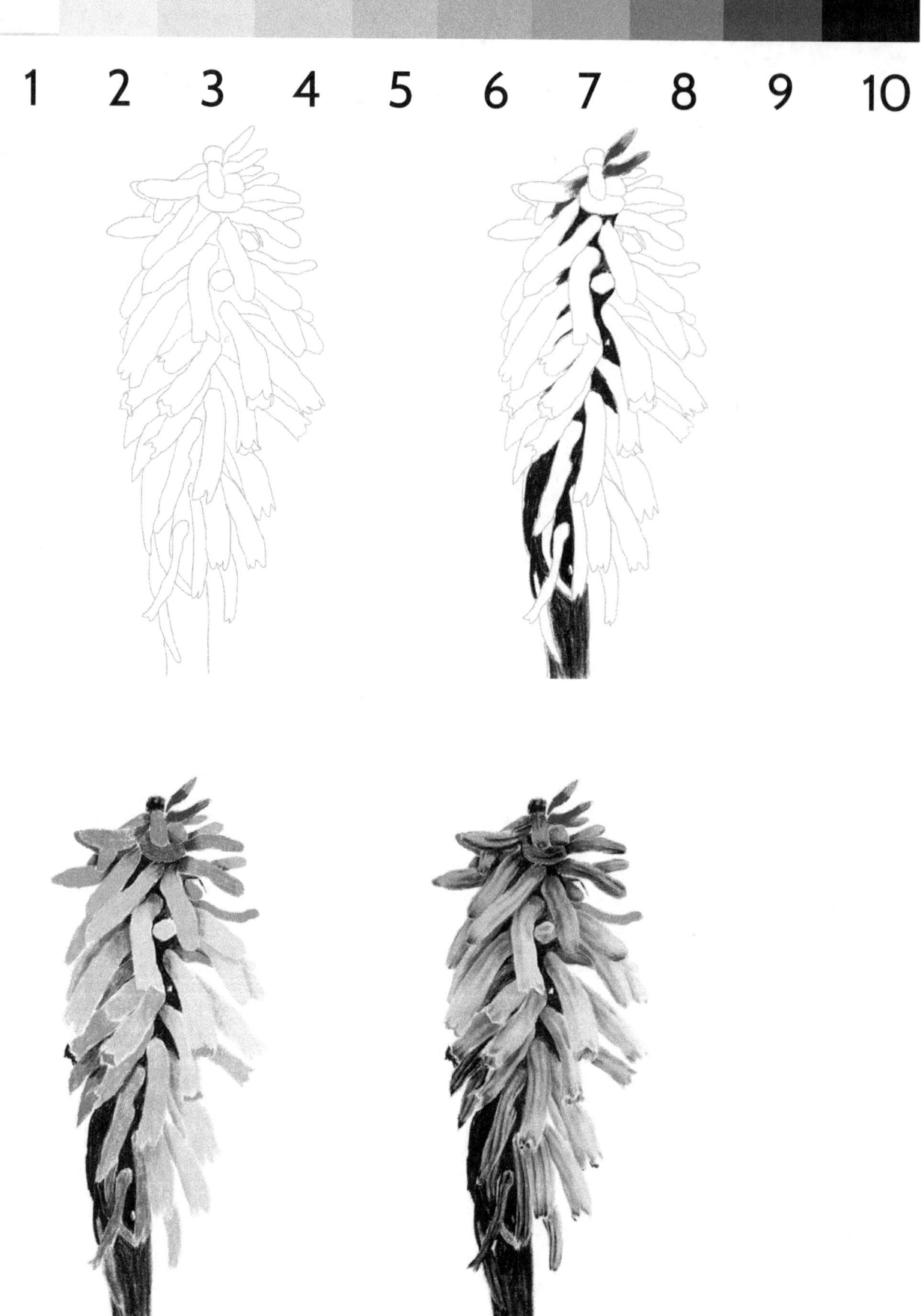

50

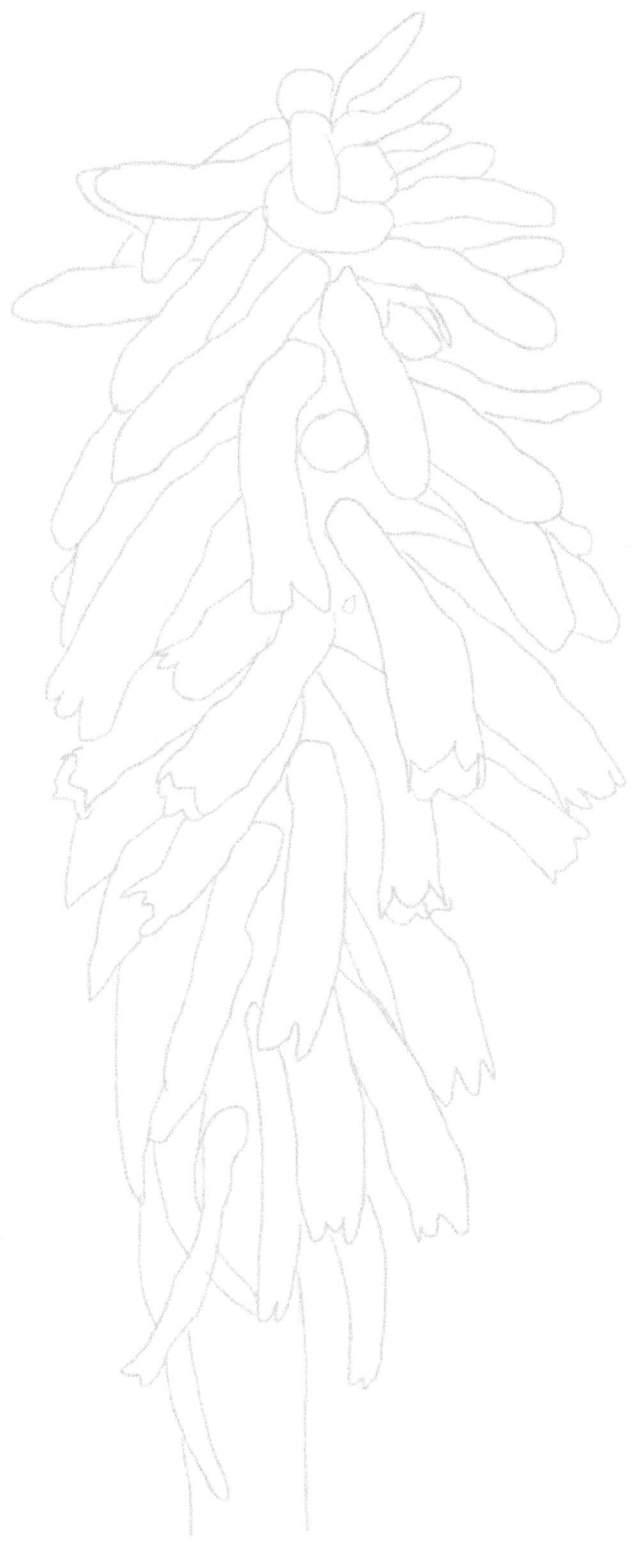

What do you call a
drawing of a clown?
A comedy Sketch

Fill In The Gaps

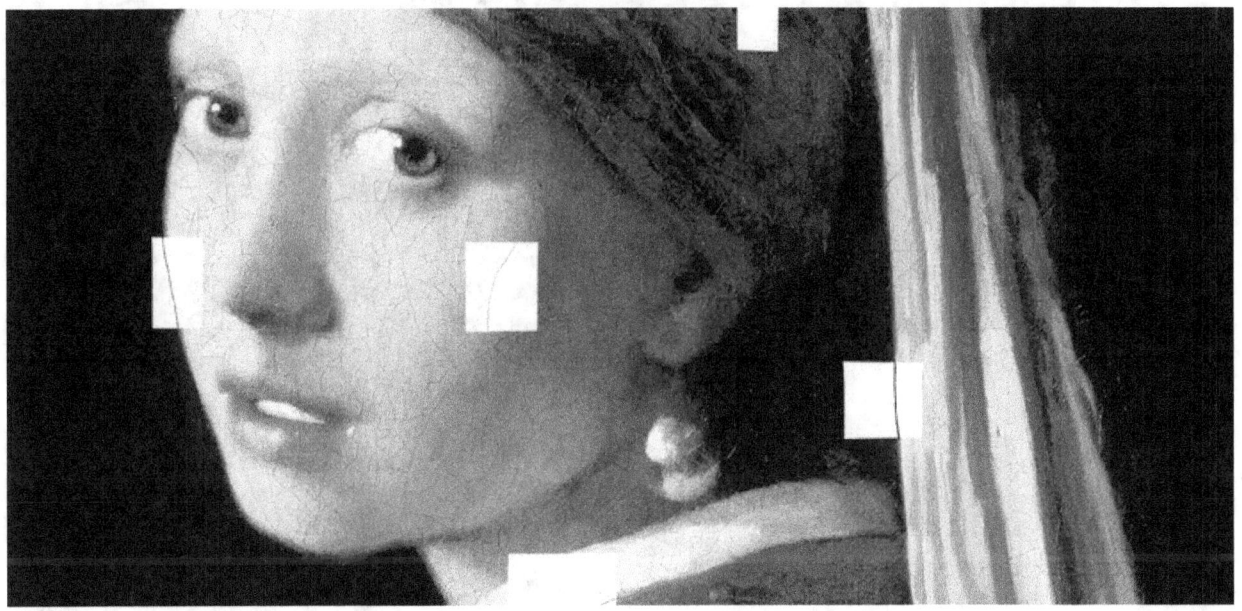

And for the final section of the book, we're going to make stuff disappear! You've done this already in this book, right at the start when you were matching the shades to the boxes. This time, there's going to be a bit of an obstacle course with some gradients and textures that you need to fill in, to make the white boxes disappear. You shouldn't be able to see any white paper and if your pencil is looking grainy, give it a sharpen and get in those little white pockets.

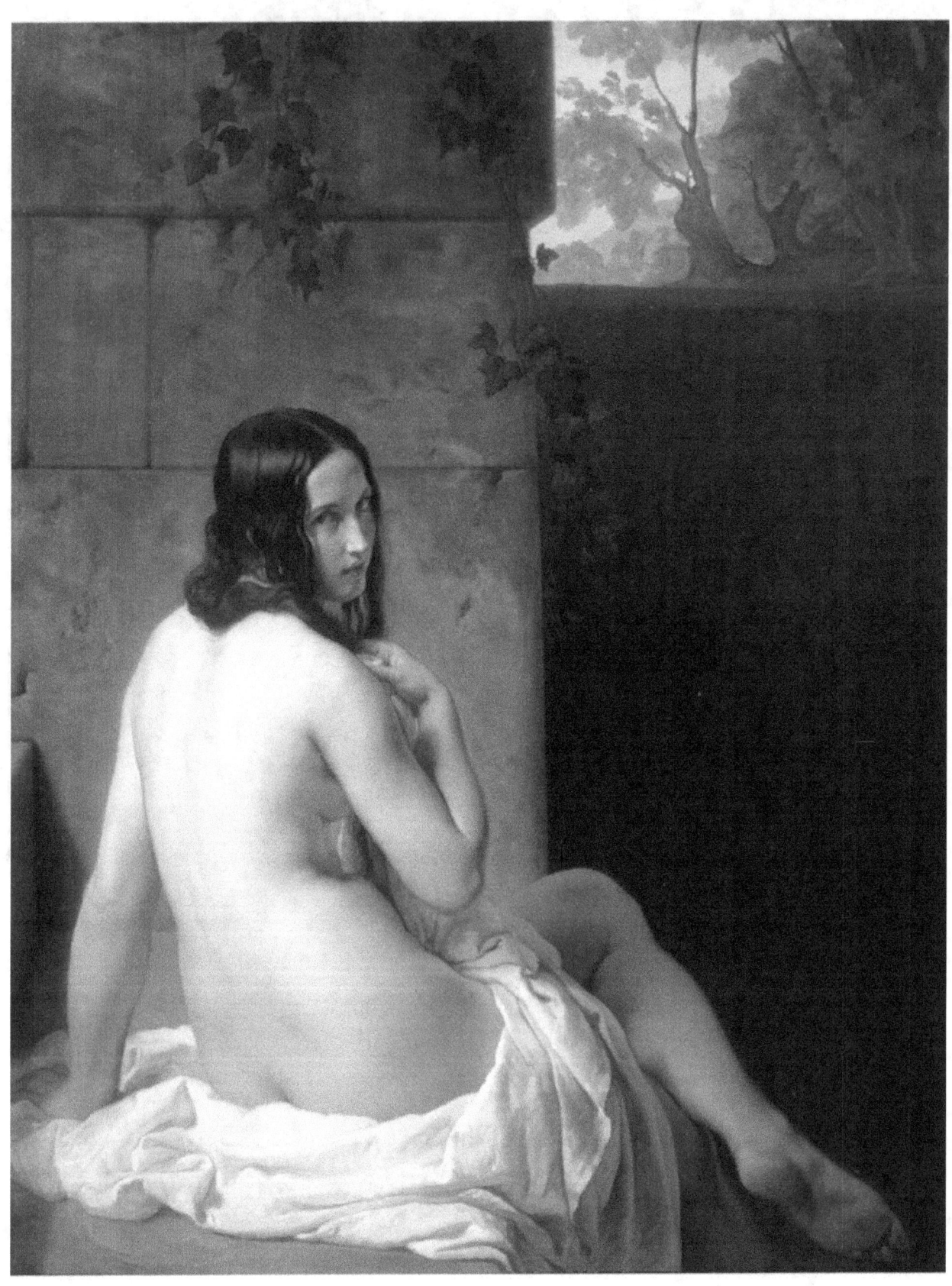

54

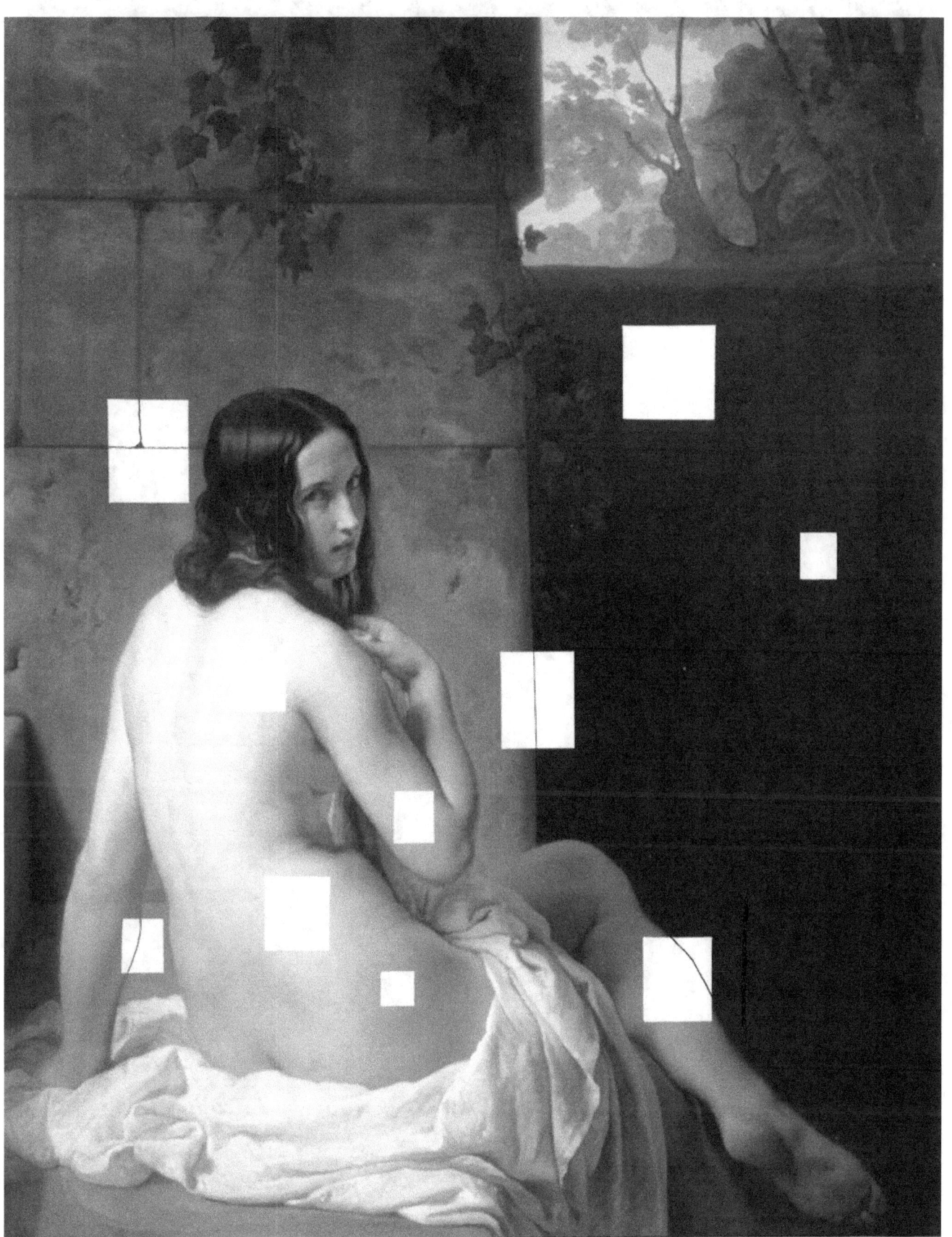

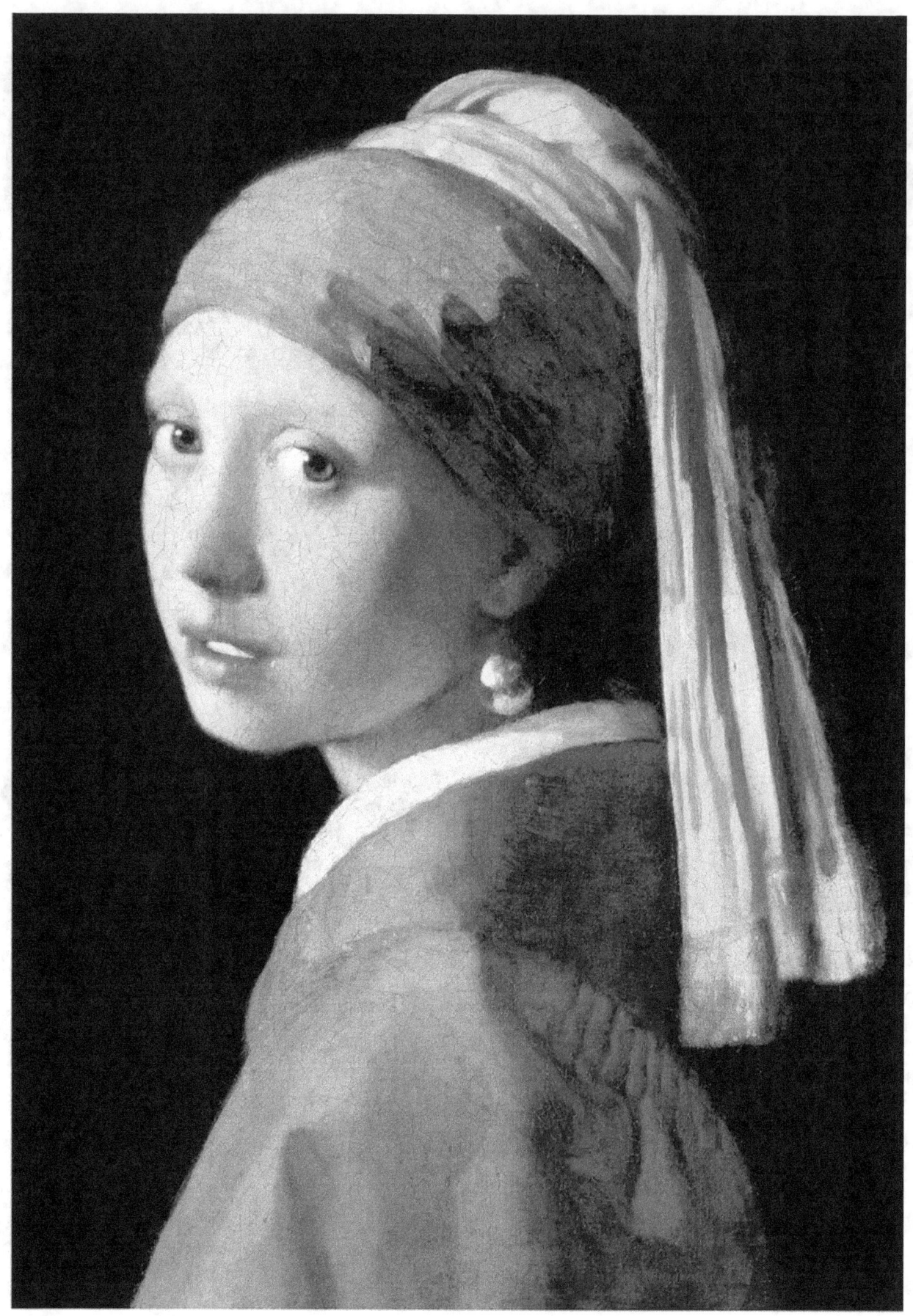

56

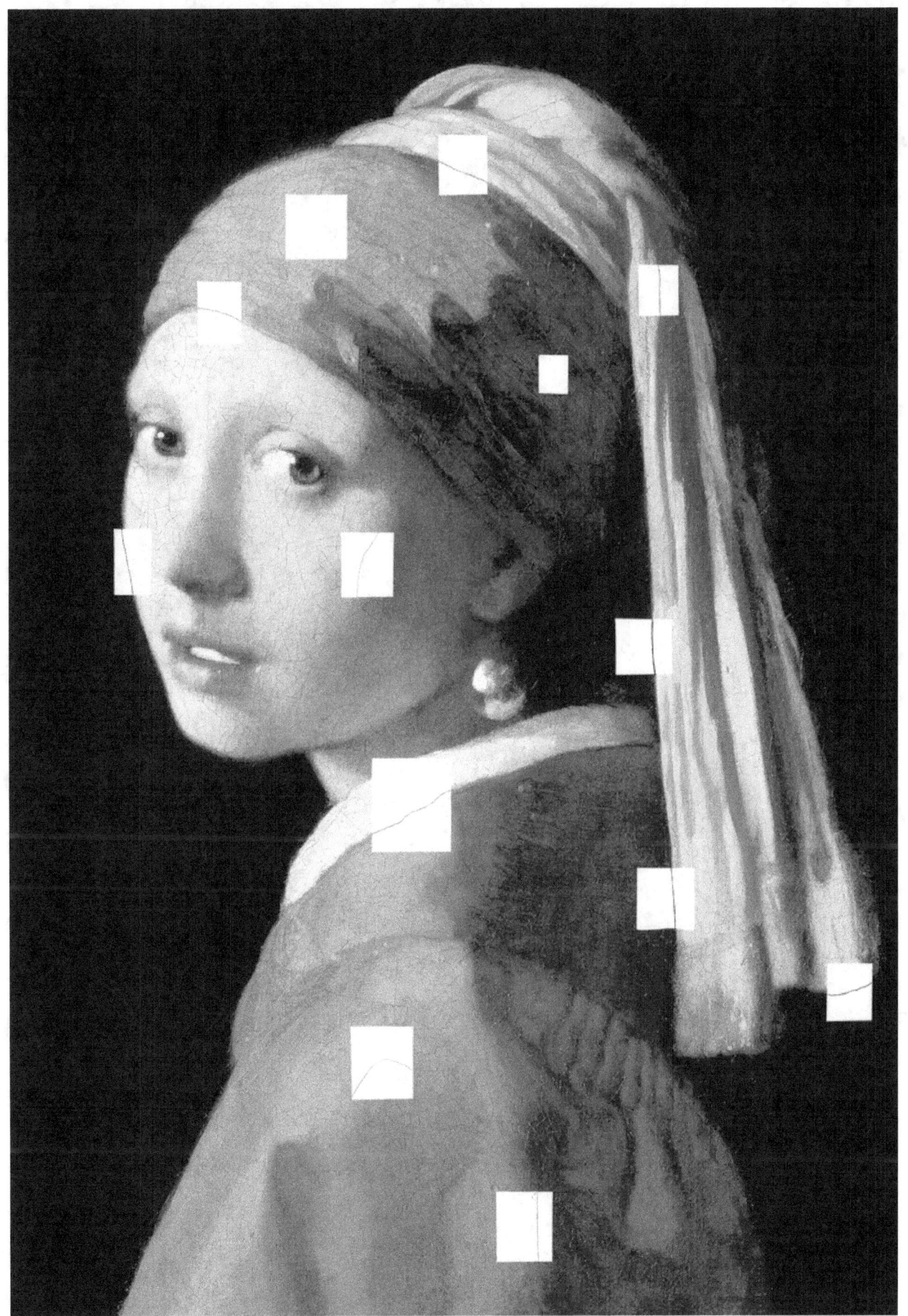

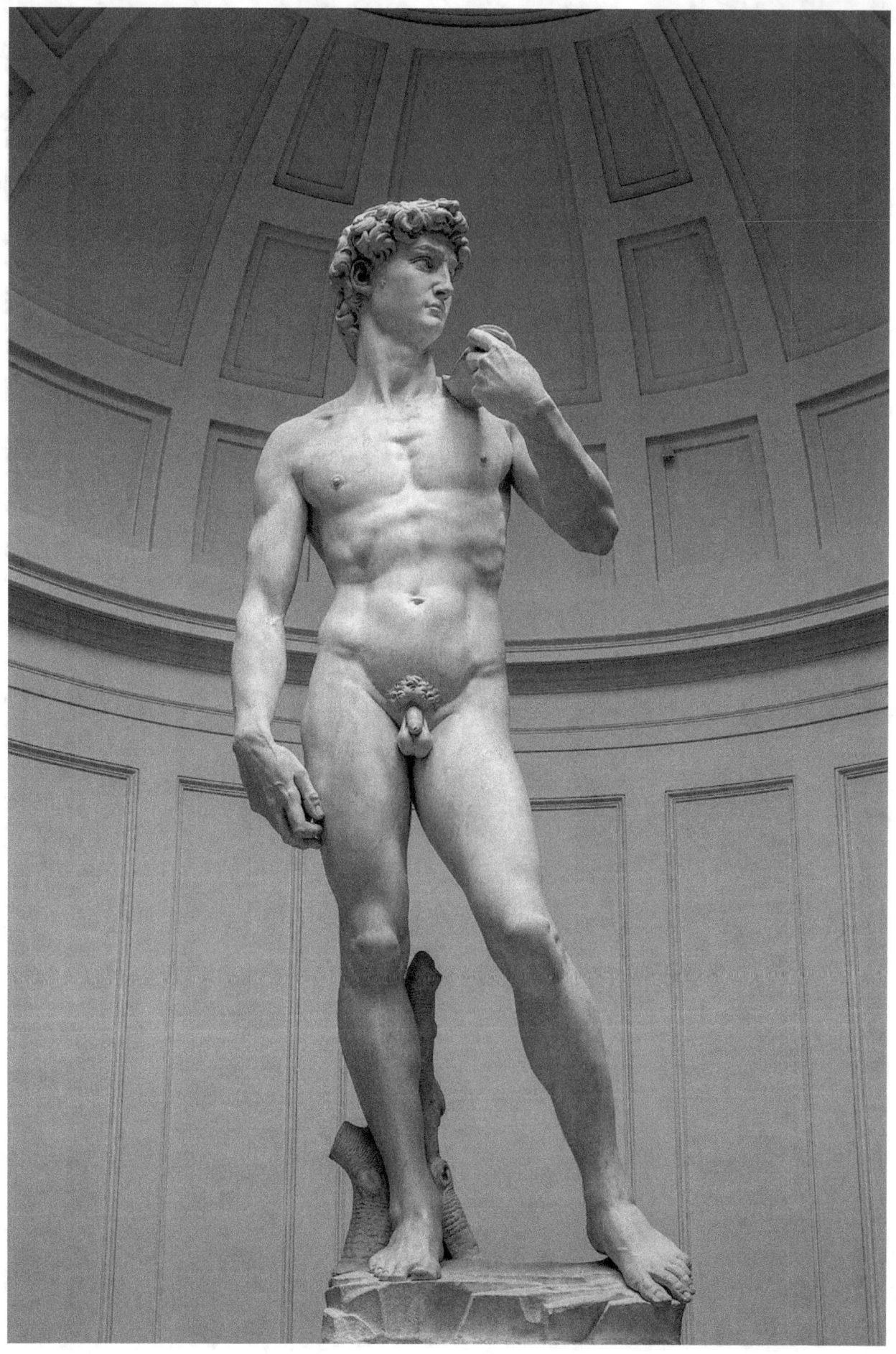

58

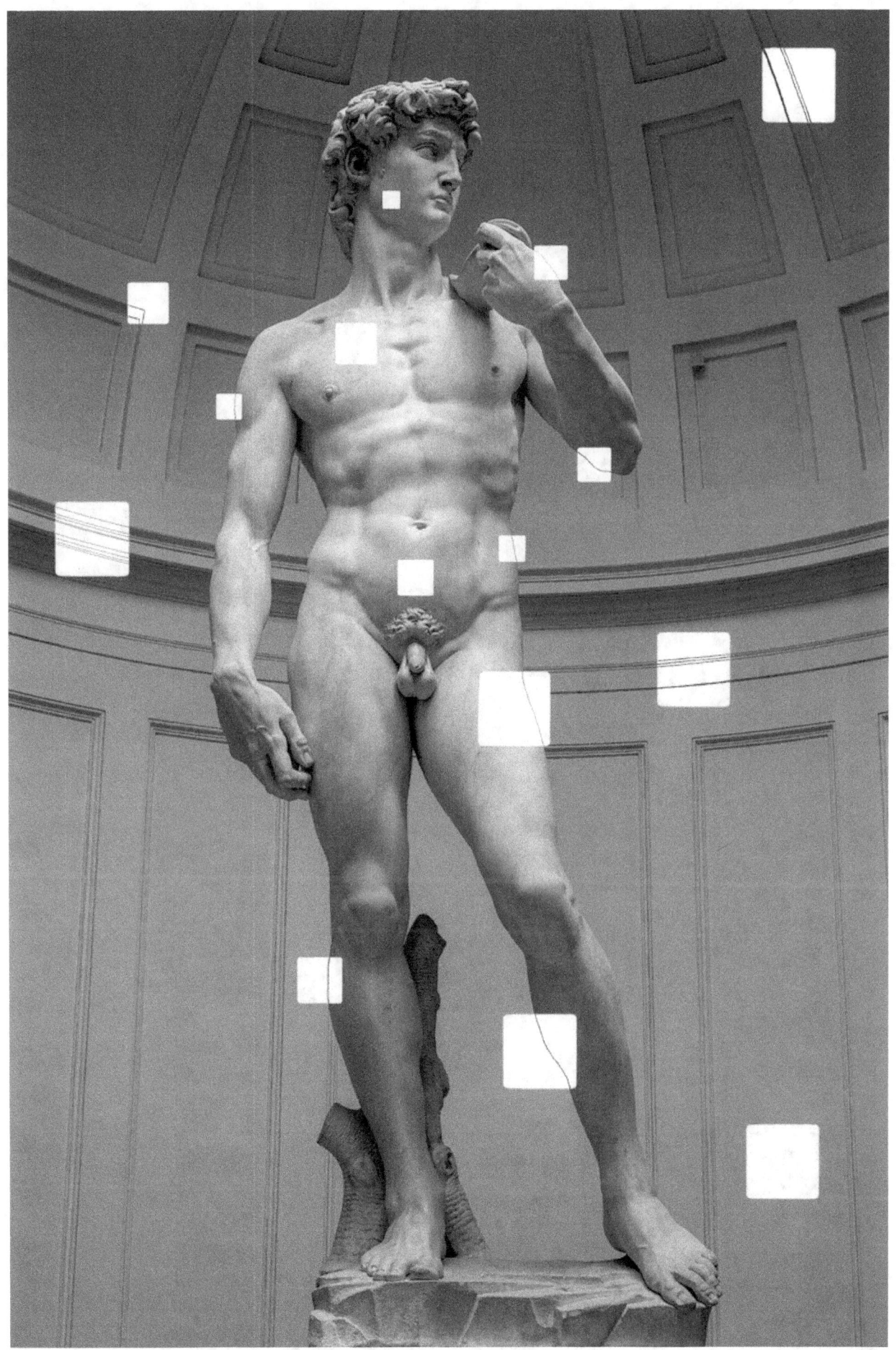

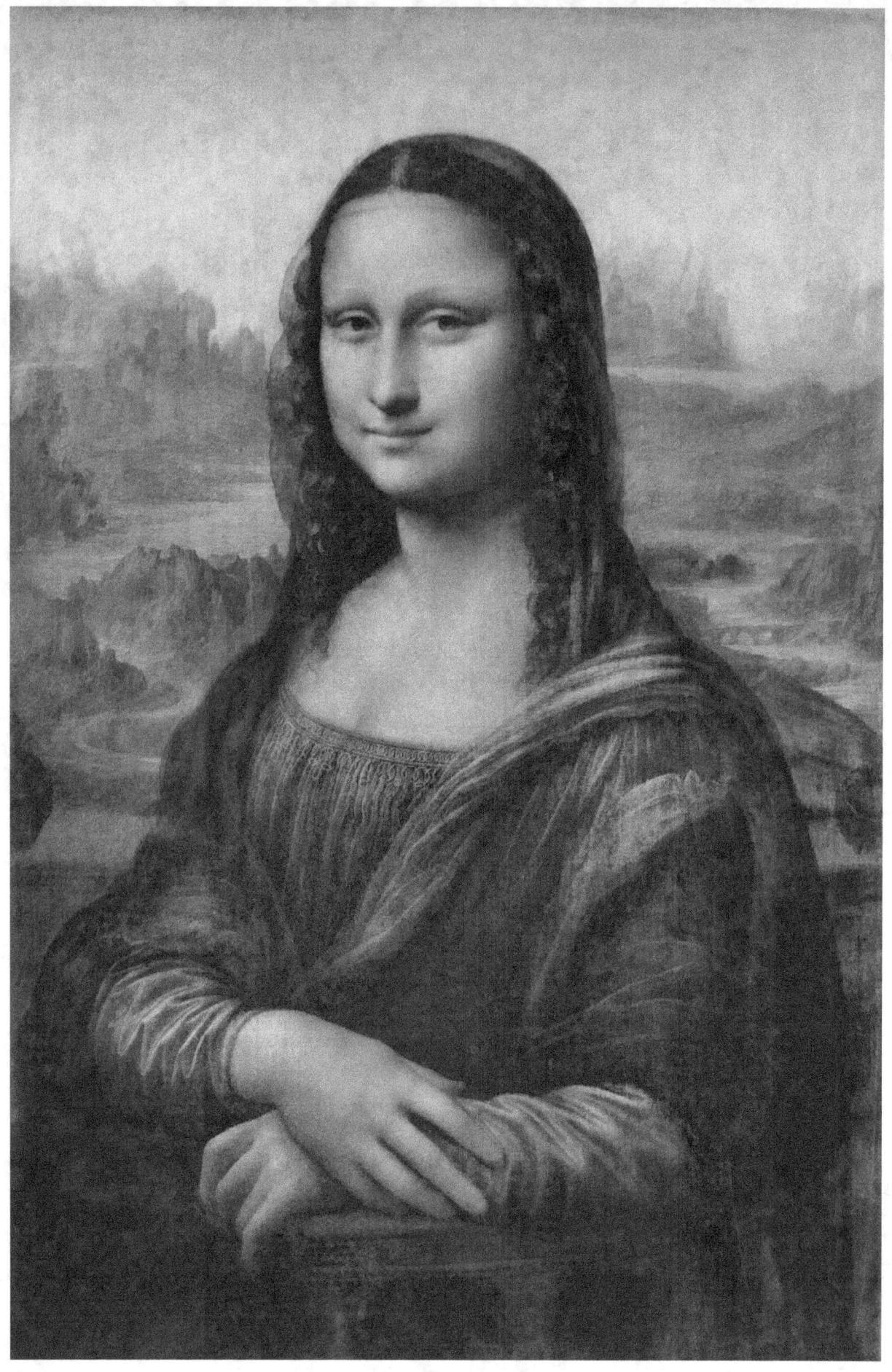

60

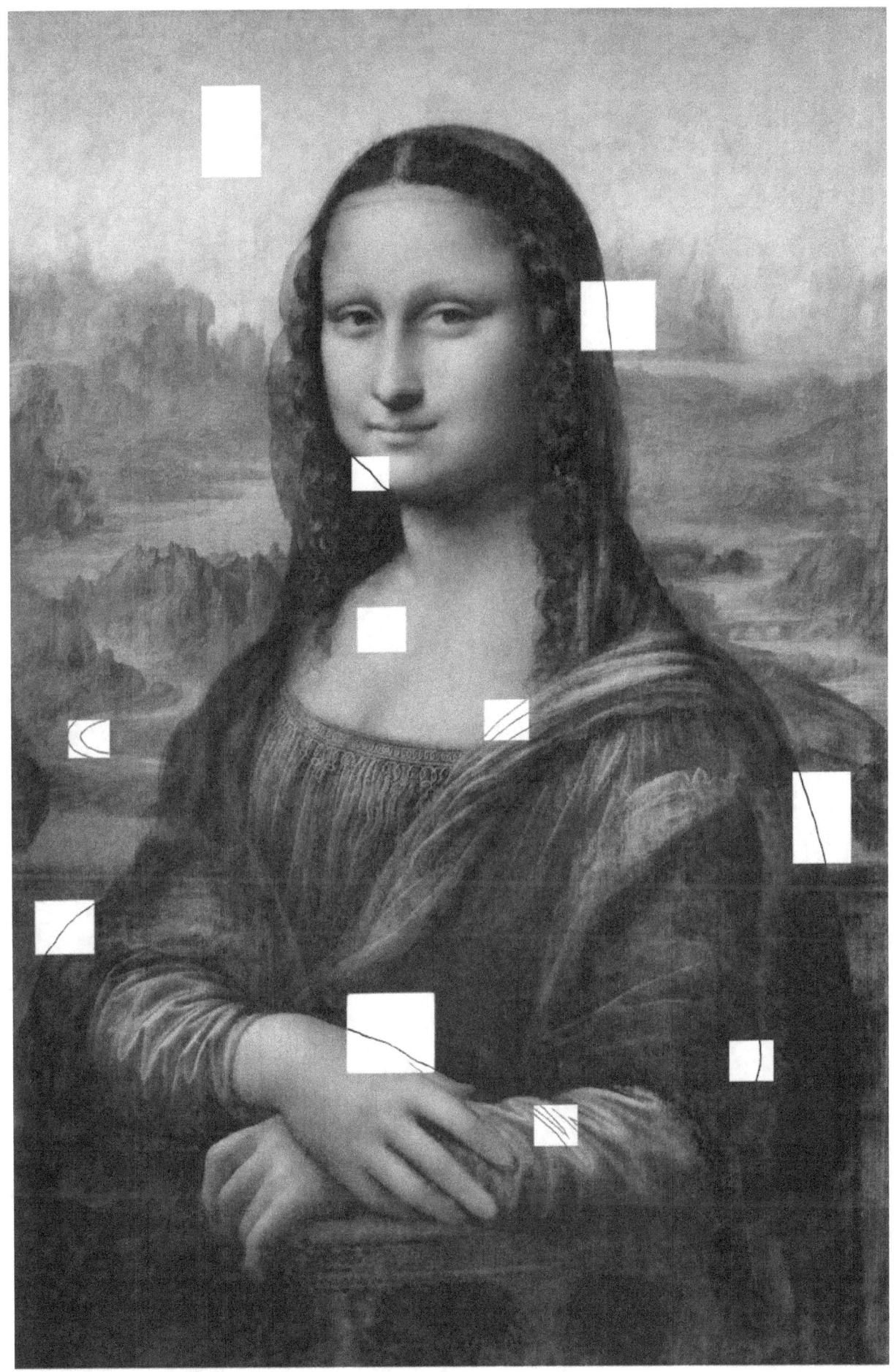

How come the artist
is in jail?
She was framed.

Well, that's all folks! Congratulations on finishing the book. I hope you enjoyed sketching and more importantly, I hope you've become mindfully addicted to shading. It's not so bad after all ey?

Thank you for shading with me and I hope our paths will cross once again. :)

Great work!

China

X

References

Answers

What Value Is This:

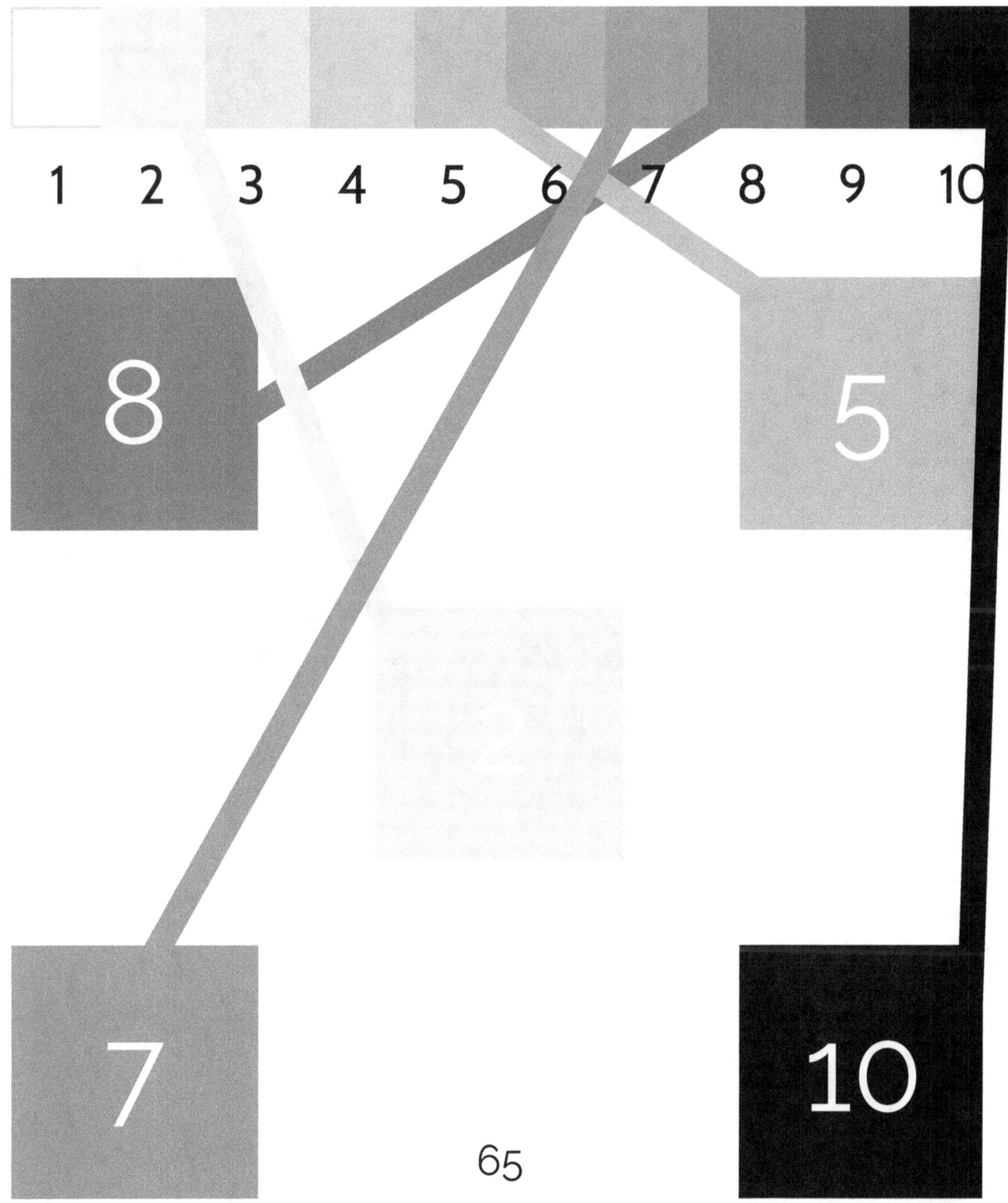

Practise Pages

If you liked this book and want to keep in touch, sign up to the mailing list by visiting the website below.

www.artistand.co.uk

Feel free to get in touch and leave any questions or feedback via email. I love hearing from my students!

china@artistand.co.uk

Finally, follow on instagram, LinkedIn & Facebook.

@ArtistAndUk